PRAISE FOR
THIRD CALLING

"Profoundly important. This book will change your life. Fresh, inspiring, and practical, *Third Calling* is destined to be a classic in the literature of purposeful living."
—**Richard Leider**, Founder of Inventure - The Purpose Company
Author of *The Power of Purpose*, *Repacking Your Bags*, and *Life Reimagined*

"As we live longer lives, it's natural to seek greater meaning and purpose as the decades unfold. Richard and Leona Bergstrom understand this imperative. Their new book, *Third Calling*, is a down-to-earth guide for people seeking to marry purpose and impact in the 'third third' of their lives. The Bergstroms understand and share the desire to make a positive difference in their communities: this book is their contribution to an important, ongoing dialogue."
—**Marc Freedman**, CEO/Founder, Encore.org
Author of *The Big Shift*, *Encore*, and *Prime Time*

"I'm convinced that life's prolonged second half will provide an opportunity for people to chart a new course. In fact, these years may be the most liberating and energizing time of their lives. *Third Calling* will challenge, encourage and inspire you to intentionally plan the rest of your life–with purpose. It is filled with personal stories, relevant research and practical tools to guide you."
—**Ken Dychtwald, Ph.D.**, President/CEO, Age Wave
Author of *A New Purpose: Redefining Money, Family, Work, Retirement and Success*

"We all know that people are living longer, but there is more to it than that. **Third Calling**, a rare gem by Richard and Leona Bergstrom, is an informative and inspiring book that offers the reader a time of conscious decision-making. Well researched, creatively developed and offering the real experiences of people, the Bergstroms provide the reader with an excellent resource that can lead to a Third Calling in life filled with clarity, hope, faith, and meaning. I highly recommend *Third Calling* as a valuable resource for anyone who is at midlife and beyond."
—**Dr. Richard H. Gentzler**, Jr., Director ENCORE Ministries, Tenn. Conference, UMC
Author of *Aging and Ministry in the 21st Century* and *Designing An Older Adult Ministry*

i

"Richard and Leona Bergstrom are leaders in Christian ministry among those exploring life's amazing second half. Their newest book, *Third Calling*, is filled with observations and ideas from Boomers inside the church, and outside as well. Each chapter offers research, insights and how-to's leading to positive and lasting outcomes. *Third Calling* brings fresh understanding and support to a restless and aging generation, still making its powerful presence felt in the church and in the world."

—Ward Tanneberg Ph.D.
Author of *Sacred Journey* and *Seasons of the Spirit*

"I am a part of the audience Richard and Leona address in *Third Calling*. I spent 25 wonderful years pastoring four different congregations and then nearly 15 years serving our denomination, Converge Worldwide. Now I am wrestling with the very questions the Bergstroms explore in their excellent book. Richard and Leona have challenged and helped a host of people, like myself, serve Christ out of a lifetime of experiences. You will be blessed by their book!"

—Dr. Jerry Sheveland, Former President of Converge Worldwide

"I come from a long line of 'non-retirees.' They saw this culture's 'retirement' as an illusion—offering little and taking much from an authentic life of purpose, influence and legacy. They did, with age, see a changing of seasons—yes. Changes in energy, strength and pace—probably. Changes in possibilities, opportunities and potential influence–NOT. As a result, my non-retiring predecessors, while having very different life stories, experienced life-long influence, productivity and fulfillment. If you find that thought both intriguing and appealing, Richard and Leona Bergstrom will help you find and follow that path, too. It's your Third Calling. And it's an amazingly important leg of your journey and mine. I highly recommend both the book—and the life."

—Dr. Bert Downs, Chancellor, Western Seminary

"*Third Calling* is Richard and Leona's life message. It's not something they simply teach and call others to. It's something they wholeheartedly live out. I've often told the two of them, 'When I grow up, I want to be like you.' As you read *Third Calling*, my hope is that something in your heart will be re-ignited—that you'll gloriously spend your entire life for Jesus until you cross to the other side of eternity."

—Jonathan Alexander, Senior Pastor,
Northshore Community Church

"*Third Calling* is one of those books that could turn your life around, bring you much joy and help you finish well. Start your Third Calling legacy by giving away copies of *Third Calling* to your Boomer friends. Your gift could spur on lasting change and fulfillment for many."

—Dr. Bruce McNicol, President, Trueface.org
Co-Author, *The Cure*

"As college students in the 70s, Richard and Leona Bergstrom were leaders among their peers, challenging them to follow God's calling in life and ministry. Decades later, they continue to inspire their generation. Their newest book, *Third Calling*, is a personal message to Boomers: 'God has designed you for a purpose for such a time as this!' Through their own life stories as well as examples from others, Richard and Leona share relevant information, helpful insights and practical ideas to help you find and follow your Third Calling. I've personally benefited from their message and I am confident you will be equally inspired."

—Teri Bradford Rouse, Senior Director, Alumni and
Parent Relations, Westmont College

"When working as a local pastor in Sweden, I noticed a change of attitude among older adults, which became a challenge to our old way of working in church. My encounter with Leona and Richard Bergstrom was a transforming experience. They expressed what I saw and offered a creative program for how to make a prospect out of what might be regarded as a threat. In their book *Third Calling*, they summarize their experiences and insights in a catchy but trustworthy manner. As a reader, you will realize that the question 'What does God want with my life?' is a very live issue to a mature person, no less than it is to a teenager."

—Anders Blåberg, General Secretary, Swedish Bible Society
Former pastor and Mission Director of Evangeliska Frikyrkan

"Aging is changing and changing fast. Most Boomers will need help in navigating the last third of life. Help has arrived. In their important book, *Third Calling*, Richard and Leona Bergstrom take you through and to your Third Calling. If you are wondering how you will spend the rest of your days, read this book!"

—Peter Menconi
Author of *The Intergenerational Church: Understanding Congregations from WWII to www.com* and *The Aging Well* Bible Study Series

"Richard and Leona Bergstrom have written a blueprint for how Boomers can find their Third Calling. With humor and seasoned wisdom from a lifetime of Christian ministry, they provide buoys that guide someone in their desire to live into their Third Calling. The process laid out in the book is an antidote to 'retirement mentality' which leads to settlers instead of a new breed of pioneers needed for the work of God around the world."

—**Jon Sween**, President, Marketplace Connections

"Richard and Leona Bergstrom exemplify the best of the Boomers. Working in ministry with Boomers, I have grown to respect and admire this couple as leaders and innovators. They are engaged and passionate. I have witnessed this couple live out strong Christ-centered convictions. They have impacted lives at workshops held at our church. Their understanding of the struggles of aging combined with their keen insight into the Boomer mindset has produced a challenging and helpful tool. Boomers facing the Third Calling will appreciate the direction provided by the Bergstroms. *Third Calling* is a resource that will be available for individuals and groups at our church."

—**Peggy Fulghum**, Boomer Ministry Director,
Johnson Ferry Baptist Church

"Richard and Leona Bergstrom wrote *Third Calling* for their peers, but it is for everyone—and, the earlier it is read, the better life will flow to its end. They masterfully, and with humor, guide the reader to identify how to live life to the fullest and avoid time wasters and traps. They help you discover how to reach true satisfaction for every day you live beyond your 'retirement' year. I will be giving many of these books as gifts to people I care about. That will be part of my legacy—giving them wisdom."

–**Elisa Hawkinson**, President, How2Organize
Author of *Calming Your Chaos: Organizing Your Life,
Home, Office and Future*

"People retire after working hard for many years. While having looked forward to it, when they actually retire they don't have a clue what to do the rest of their lives. Some sit on the couch, twiddle their thumbs and pretty soon, you're reading their obituary. We shouldn't be surprised because the Bible warned us, 'Where there is no vision, the people perish.' Richard and Leona Bergstrom aim to change that. *Third Calling* is about giving Boomers a formula to discover and carry out a new vision for the rest of their lives."

–**Dr. Robert Anderson**, President, Masters Tours
Former Professor of Pastoral Theology, Western Seminary
Author of *The Effective Pastor: A Practical Guide to Ministry*

"As a Marriage and Family Therapist, I often reflect on how the members of our society are dying for lack of meaning. We see people of all ages who have a plethora of things, entertainment and opportunities and yet are depressed, anxious and often suicidal. Our society promises fulfillment through beauty, wealth and fame but all that results is hollowness and disappointment. Many work tirelessly toward retirement thinking that then 'the good life' begins, never realizing that the 'good life' is not found in doing less but is found in purpose and meaning; in doing for others and making a difference—and responding to God's calling. *Third Calling*, by Richard and Leona Bergstrom, not only demonstrates this point but also guides us through the process, pointing us again toward the true meaning and rewards in life. I hope many of us in the Boomer generation will respond to their invitation to explore how to jump into this next stage with anticipation—especially those who because of society's pressure and false promises have not had the opportunity to follow their hearts and live a life of meaning."

—**Donelyn Miller, LMFT**, Co-Owner, Relational Resources
Counseling Center
Adjunct Professor, Western Seminary

"In this inspiring book, Richard and Leona Bergstrom share Biblical insights, glimpses of their journey and stories of others embracing their Third Calling. Thought provoking and practical, it helps the reader examine the questions, 'Who am I?' 'Why am I here?' 'What's my purpose?' 'How do I embrace it?' A must read for those seeking meaning and purpose in this season of life."

—**Richard Pearce**, Co-Founder, Fresh Horizons,
Churches of Christ Australia

"Just when you're tempted to think life is winding down, the Bergstroms rattle your world and convince you that it's winding UP. And you've got a whole new calling, something significant to do for the rest of your life."

—**Marshall Shelley**, Director, Doctor of Ministry Program,
Denver Seminary
Former editor, Leadership Journal; Contributing Editor,
Christianity Today's CT Pastors.org

"*Third Calling* is a powerful, practical resource for Boomers seeking a positive direction toward life's later seasons. The Bergstroms offer wise counsel to enlighten, encourage and challenge us on this exciting path, helping us grasp Kingdom potential in a deeper way."

—**Wes Wick**, Director/Co-Founder, YES! Young Enough to Serve

"Our most important assets are not what we have in the bank but the life assets we accumulate on the journey of living. Richard and Leona's book, *Third Calling*, helps you identify and focus those assets in high-potential, fulfilling ways. It's a great handbook for what may be your most productive and rewarding years."

—**Phill Butler**, Founder and Senior Strategic Advisor, visionSynergy
Author of *Well Connected: Releasing Power,*
Restoring Hope through Kingdom Partnerships

"If you are over 50 and have been struggling, frustrated, and stressed about your next steps in life, *Third Calling* is a MUST-read for you. Leona and Richard have created a book that helps answer the great questions we are all asking: 'Who am I?' 'Why am I here?' and 'What am I to do with the rest of this wild and wonderful life?'"

—**Rev. Charles McKinney**, Pastor to Boomers and Senior Adults,
First Baptist Church Jacksonville

"Richard and Leona Bergstrom have brilliantly, Biblically and expertly written a book for Boomers wanting purpose and meaning as well as seeking the tools and skills necessary to navigate this new season. I highly recommend *Third Calling* to those who now find themselves with both memories and dreams!"

—**John Coulombe**, interGen Pastor, First Evangelical Free
Church of Fullerton

"*Third Calling* is more than just a book to be read—it is a powerful map and guided tour for Boomers, designed to help them realize the power they have in this new season to still be 'World Changers.' It is a tremendous work—well researched and incredibly practical. The Bergstroms have given each of us Boomers a wonderful gift. A gift such as this one should not be missed."

—**Dr. Chuck Stecker**, Executive Director and Founder
A Chosen Generation & The Center for interGenerational Ministry
Author of *Men of Honor, Women of Virtue: The Power of Rites of Passage*
into Godly Adulthood

THIRD CALLING

What are you doing the rest of your life?

Richard & Leona Bergstrom

THIRD CALLING: What are you doing the rest of your life?

Published by:
Re-Ignite, a division of ChurchHealth
www.Re-Ignite.net
www.ThirdCalling.com
www.CHonline.org

Richard and Leona Bergstrom
P.O. Box 1493
Edmonds, Washington 98020
Email: info@chonline.org

Unless otherwise noted, Scripture quotations are taken from The Holy Bible, New International Version. © 1973, 1978, 1984 International Bible Society. Used by permission of Zondervan Bible Publishers.

The Message, Eugene Peterson. Published by NavPress. 2007.

English Standard Version, Crossway Bible. 2001.

New Living Translation, Tyndale House. 2006.

Holman Christian Standard Bible, BH Publishing. 2010

Worldwide English Bible, SOON Educational Publishers. 1996

ISBN: 978-0-9705552-1-2

Editors: Susan Hedding and Paul Muncey
Cover design: Scott Bothel, FourTen Creative
Back cover photo: Jeff Dils, Zephyr Images
Interior Book Layout: Paul Muncey and Susan Hedding

Every attempt has been made to properly source all quotes.

Printed in the United States of America.
First Edition

Dedicated to our grandchildren
Noah, Graham, Brinley,
Nolan, Finley, Maya

"The Lord will keep you from all harm—
he will watch over your life;
the Lord will watch over your coming and going
both now and forevermore."
Psalm 121:7-8

CONTENTS

FOREWORD

For the past twenty years I have devoted myself to ministry with older adults and specifically ministry with the aging Baby Boomer. Whether it be in my research as a gerontologist, my consulting with churches, or speaking with Boomers themselves, one thing is certain, Baby Boomers are different. (Grin!) Not only is this group unique because of their sheer size (78 million strong) but throughout their lives they have radically shaped society.

Typically defined as being born between 1946-1964, Boomers have been described as independent, cause-oriented, and well-educated. As Boomers age, they are interested in work, even if that means part-time work or volunteer work. They want to stay young and active, all while juggling many responsibilities. Contrary to what popular culture may tell us, Boomers are dealing with a number of life stresses such as caring for aging parents, relating to adult children, navigating health challenges and being involved with their grandchildren. They are not interested in being called a 'senior' nor are they content to simply retire to the rocking chair on the front porch or attend a potluck luncheon.

Boomers care about social justice issues as well as being a positive influence in their own family and community. This generation wants to leverage their life to make a difference. Perhaps this describes you. You want your life to count. You want to know that your passions matter. You want to utilize your life experience for something good. But you just aren't sure how. That is the purpose of this book.

Third Calling is Biblically-based, challenging and very practical. In these pages, you will be inspired to discover your own Third Calling. You will hear the motivational stories of ordinary people like you, who have discovered their purpose and are living it out. You will explore your strengths, abilities and even uncover the key events in your life that have shaped who you are today and how God wants to use you in the years ahead.

Richard and Leona Bergstrom are some of the best field guides I know to help us on this journey of discovery. Having known them for nearly 20 years, they not only bring years of education, ministry experience and expertise, but more importantly they are leading-edge Baby Boomers themselves and are living out their own Third Calling. They have been willing to downsize their home and possessions, leave a comfortable job and follow their passion in order to make their life count! Throughout this book you will see how their story intertwines with what God wants to do through your own life story. You will find yourself saying, "I should do this! I can do this! I will do this!"

When I wrote my book, *Baby Boomers and Beyond,* one of my greatest desires was to encourage church leaders to respond to the huge army of adults that God was raising up. A group of people moving into the retirement season of their lives with time, experience and resources. People who are often untapped, yet full of potential for making a Kingdom impact with their lives. You are among those people. You may question what you have to offer at this season in your life. You may be tempted to believe the lies that you are too old to make a change or too old to learn something new. You may have even tried to give of yourself only to be told you weren't needed. Regardless of what you have believed, the truth is you are needed! Your family, your neighborhood, your church, and the world desperately need what you have to offer. God has a unique purpose to fulfill through you. So, what are you waiting for? Dive into the pages of this book and then engage in your Third Calling!

Amy Hanson, Ph.D.
www.amyhanson.org
author of *Baby Boomers and Beyond:
Tapping the Ministry Talents and Passions of Adults over 50*

PREFACE

By Leona

"Sometimes it falls upon a generation to be great.
You can be that great generation."
—Nelson Mandela

THE TIME IS NOW

Third Calling is a message to every person in our generation.

We, the authors, are Boomers. Born in the 1950s, we belong to a great generation recognized for its size, strength and attitude. Historically known for being counter-cultural, we have challenged society's expectations for how we act, believe, vote, and now, how we will age. Standing on the threshold of a new season of life we, as individuals within a generation, can consider the opportunities, confront the prevalent assumptions and embrace a fresh calling and purpose.

Throughout this book, we establish the case that each one of us is uniquely created and designed for a purpose–for such a time as this. We have rich and diverse life experiences. We care deeply about a broad scope of issues, causes and people. We are here, at this place in time, for a reason. Never before has a generation had such an opportunity to redefine this time of life. We have the responsibility to steward it well.

We define stages in life as: First Calling–the challenges of young adulthood; Second Calling–the responsibilities of midlife;

and Third Calling–the opportunities of maturity. It's a new stage, a blank canvas we can fill with color, action and story. It is time to engage in our Third Calling.

In 2010, we founded **Re-Ignite**, a ministry designed to encourage our peers, the Boomers, to re-ignite passion and purpose in life, work and ministry—and even in retirement. Our aim is to see individuals transformed by discovering what God wants them to do in the next chapter of their lives. Our hope is that Christians will discover and follow their Third Calling. Our dream is, ideas will come alive, needs will be met, issues resolved, generations will work together, and the world will change.

A NEW MODEL: THIRD CALLING

We propose an entirely new paradigm and name for this season and adventure we call aging. We implore individuals, and our entire generation, to consider a Third Calling:

> *"You never change things by fighting the existing reality.*
> *To change something, build a new model that*
> *makes the existing model obsolete."*
> —Richard Buckminster Fuller
> Architect and Inventor

THE PREMISE

Long life is a gift from God, to be stewarded with wisdom and imagination. Every mature person must discover his or her unique design, passion and purpose in life and follow their Third Calling.

THE PARTICIPANTS

Third Calling people are those, who are willing to move, to dance. They aren't afraid to follow and they are not timid to lead. They are ready to boogie.

Third Calling people are leading-edge Boomers. They are the "Do-Bees," kids of the 50s and 60s, revolutionaries, and some hippies. They are called to something more than a life of only play and leisure; they are ready to change the world.

Third Calling people are people of faith. They believe in God, his mission and his people.

THE PLAN

Third Calling people are transformed. As a result of discovering their Third Calling, they've changed–from the inside out.

Third Calling people are engaged. They find a need and meet it. They tap into their outrage, compassion and convictions and find ways to serve. They connect with others and work together to meet spiritual and social needs. They inform and educate those of all ages and generations about the gift of long life.

Third Calling people mobilize others in their communities and churches to subvert the dominant paradigm of aging and maturity. They are advocates.

THE PRINCIPLES

To be a person who embraces your Third Calling and works with others to fuel a movement, we believe you should consider following the principles we discuss in the book:

- Follow your calling and what you believe God wants you to do in this season of life. (Chapter 1, 2)
- Understand your own story and how God has used people, events and circumstances to shape you into the person you are today. (Chapter 4)
- Take time to discover what makes you unique: your values, personality, strengths, motivations, spiritual gifts, purpose, passion and dreams. (Chapters 3, 5, 6, 7, 8)

- Walk closely with God and listen to his leading. (Chapter 11)
- Nurture creative thinking, explore new worlds, begin new enterprises and start taking risks. (Chapters 9, 10, 12, 13)
- Embrace the challenges and difficulties in this season of life.(Chapter 14)
- Make a plan for how you will see your Third Calling become a reality. Bring people alongside you for help and support. (Chapters 15, 16)
- Understand the dominant cultural attitude toward aging and resist it. (Chapter 17, 18)
- Be a leader in your Third Calling. Live a legacy. (Chapter 19)

"If your actions inspire others to dream more,
learn more, do more and become more, you are a leader."
—John Quincy Adams

THE PROPOSAL

As each one of us embraces our Third Calling, we can walk hand in hand with those of all generations, seeking to make the world a better, more loving place–all for God's glory, and ultimately, for His purpose.

Are you ready to discover and follow your Third Calling?
If so, you are joining a movement.
You are leading the change.

"The secret of change is to focus all of your energy,
not on fighting the old, but on building the new."
—Socrates

Blessings on Your Third Calling,
Richard Bergstrom, D.Min.
and Leona Bergstrom
Authors, *Third Calling: What are you doing the rest of your life?*
Co-Founders/Co-Directors, Re-Ignite
www.Re-Ignite.net
www.ThirdCalling.com

PART ONE:
YOUR THIRD CALLING

CHAPTER 1

POPPING THE QUESTION

What are you doing the rest of your life?

by Leona

"I knew when I met you an adventure was going to happen."
—Winnie the Pooh, A.A. Milne

*"Call to me and I will answer you and tell you great
and unsearchable things you do not know."*
—Jeremiah 33:3

FEW PEOPLE KNEW ABOUT THE little room adjacent to the main lounge in my college residence hall. Since I was a Resident Assistant in that dorm, I frequently escaped there to find space and solitude. On December 7, 1971, Richard and I met there to "talk," or as college students would say, "define the relationship."

We had dated for nearly two years and were crazy about each other. We were pretty sure it was love because we couldn't stand being apart. We tried separation for the three days leading up to this meeting, but we were both insufferably miserable.

We sat on a broken vinyl sofa and talked, argued a little and shed a few tears. Then Richard did what any smart, perceptive young man would do. He got down on one knee and asked me to marry him. Whew. Marriage—rich or poor, sick or well, happy or sad— forever, 'til death do us part. How hard could that be? Of course, I said yes.

Our perfect stillness was accompanied only by the sounds of our loudly beating hearts until we noticed someone playing the grand piano out in the main room. We recognized the song: *What Are You Doing the Rest of Your Life?*[1]

Since then we've debated whether hearing the song was a sign, coincidence or, as Richard maintains, "a perfectly planned background." We revisit the song every anniversary and have the words posted on a plaque in our home.

"What are you doing the rest of your life?" was a clarifying question for us decades ago when we considered marriage and our future. It was the beginning of a new season of life we call our First Calling. During this period, we pursued education, got married, started a career and had two babies twenty-two months apart. We moved a few times and eventually bought a Ford station wagon and took out a home mortgage. "What are you doing the rest of your life?" was full of newness, unending potential and a lot of stress.

Somewhere along the way, we began hitting our stride. We both worked in defined careers, Richard in full-time ministry and I in health care administration. Our kids were involved in school, sports and youth group. We had a cat and a dog. We drove a minivan. We moved a few times and changed jobs more than once, but we were relatively settled into "midlife" or what we define as our Second Calling. We periodically revisited the question, "What are you doing the rest of your life?," but mostly we just kept surviving, maintaining our family, jobs and our credit score.

Then, all too soon, the kids left home, married and began living their lives on their own. We downsized our possessions and bought a red Mustang convertible. We became grandparents— six times in six years. And, we began asking questions about the meaning of it all. What was our purpose in this stage of life? What compelled us to get up in the morning?

We turned the age when people expected us to "retire." We realized we were entering an entirely new and uncharted season. Refusing to go quietly into the night, we sensed it was time for a new direction, a new beginning, a new purpose and passion. We entered our Third Calling,

The words to "our" song became foundational to this new season: "What are you doing the rest of your life?" The answers to that question guide and direct us every single day.

How about you? Have you survived the first two callings through adulthood? Have you accomplished family and career goals? Have you experienced a wake-up call that has jolted you from thinking life would last forever? Are you ready to consider what's next?

We have written this book is to encourage you in the discovery of what God wants you to be and do for the rest of your life. We are writing it together because the message is from both of our hearts and minds. We've added bylines after each chapter title so you will know who is writing. We are speaking from the context of our own life journey, which is shaped by our commitment to follow Jesus Christ. In each chapter, we will introduce you to others from many walks of life and worldviews, who have searched for meaning and purpose.

We invite you to join us in the adventure.

Discover your Third Calling!

Consider: What event or life circumstance is transitioning you into your Third Calling?

CHAPTER 2
FOLLOWING THE CALL
by Richard

"Every calling is great when greatly pursued."
—Oliver Wendall Holmes

"Live a life worthy of the calling you have received."
—Ephesians 4:1

IN BRIGHT, COLORFUL FONTS AND designs, Westmont College's website invites you to "Live Your Calling." Their message is geared to young adults in their 20s who are living in their First Calling. Sounds exciting, doesn't it? Having the opportunity to be and do exactly what you are uniquely designed for—every day of your life? It almost seems unimaginable.

As we begin this book, we explain how you can follow and live your Third Calling. We show you how to define who you are, and how to identify what you care about and what your life's purpose is. As the great Christian philosopher, Francis Schaeffer reminds us, "When we understand our calling, it is not only true, but beautiful—and it should be exciting."[1]

Westmont—our college alma mater located in Santa Barbara, California—offers some profound insights about knowing, following and living your calling. They apply to those of us in our Third Calling as much as to college students. Their definition of calling is: "a strong urge toward a particular way of life or career; a vocation." They go on to explain, "There is a calling on our lives.

God has called us into his Kingdom and to be participants in his work in the world. It is the on-going task of every Christian to discern the shape of that calling through the various phases of life." [2]

While the Office of Career Development and Calling helps students write resumes and secure internships, they also encourage going deeper to explore critical components of finding your calling, such as personality, strengths, motivations, values, and passions. Those of us in our Third Calling need to do likewise.

It is significant to note the three aspects of calling outlined on Westmont's website:

- First, *God has called us into his Kingdom,* and
- Second, *to be participants in his work in the world.*
- Third, *It is the ongoing task of every Christian to discern the shape of that calling through the various phases of life.*

Let's examine them more closely in light of our Third Calling.

The first aspect of the statement is: *God has called us into his Kingdom.* This implies a call to faith in Christ. We become a part of God's family when we believe that Jesus is the Son of God, who died and rose again to save us from sin. We respond to God's first call in our lives by choosing to follow Jesus Christ. It is our call "to be," to abide in Christ.

The New Testament is filled with stories of men and women who personally heard Jesus' voice bidding them to "come." Sometimes it was a simple, "Follow me," such as Jesus' call to the fishermen, Peter, Andrew, James and John (Luke 5). The Bible says they put down their nets and followed him immediately. Others took a bit more urging and explanation. Nicodemus needed clarity about what it meant to be born again (John 3); Paul needed a dramatic revelation (Acts 9), and Martha needed to be still and listen (Luke 10). Each of us needs to hear the Caller, respond to, and follow him.

Being a part of God's Kingdom implies obedience to the King. Followers of Christ recognize the authority of the Master in their lives. They take seriously the exhortation of the Apostle Paul in Scripture "to live a life worthy of their calling." That includes such instructions as to "love one another," "pray for those who persecute you," "forgive those who wrong you," "give to those in need," "honor your father and mother," "do not steal," "do not covet," "do not commit adultery," "be prepared to share about your hope in Christ," and hundreds of other commands. As Jesus prepared to leave this earth, he gave his followers one final command, referred to as the Great Commission, when he said, "Therefore go and make disciples of all nations, baptizing them in the name of the Father and of the Son and of the Holy Spirit, and teaching them to obey everything I have commanded you." [3]

The second aspect of the statement is: *to be participants in his work in the world.* Each Christian has a *calling* that has to do with what God is directing him or her to accomplish in life. Historically that is what is referred to as our *vocation*. "At first, vocation was understood to mean that everyone is called to both salvation and service, without a clergy-laity divide." [4] But as Os Guinness points out, "Catholics had for centuries suggested there were 'two ways of life' for the church. The 'perfect life,' or the spiritual one, dedicated to contemplation and reserved for monks and nuns; as opposed to 'the permitted life,' or the secular." Guinness continues, "Protestants had made a similar mistake in elevating the secular at the expense of the spiritual, and reducing vocation to an alternative word for work. Slowly such words as *work, trade, employment*, and *occupation* came to be used interchangeably with calling and vocation. (But) for Martin Luther, the peasant and the merchant can do God's work (or fail to do it) just as much as the minister and the missionary." [5]

I entered college in the fall of 1969 with a clear sense of calling to pastoral ministry. My church in Phoenix even acknowledged those of us with a call to "vocational Christian ministry" as "Christian Service Students" and followed us through our education all the way to our ordination to the ministry. In my early years of ministry I didn't always recognize the fact that a businessperson, a homemaker, or a person in the trades might have a calling as distinct as those of us called to "the ministry." I was committed to my pastoral calling to "equip the saints for the work of the ministry,"[6] but all too often that was focused on helping them find their place of service in the church.

Today, however, I recognize that each one of us has a sacred calling upon our lives. The call to serve as a pastor, a teacher or a missionary is no more sacred or important than that of a businessperson, homemaker, mechanic, farmer, or doctor. We participate in Christ's work in the world by following our calling.

"Your calling is where your own greatest joy
intersects with the needs of the world."
—Frederick Buechner

The third aspect of the Westmont statement is: *It is the ongoing task of every Christian to discern the shape of that calling through the various phases of life.*

The expression of your calling may change as you face transitions in the third–third of your life. We use the terms First, Second and Third Calling to define our life in stages. Whether you have spent your working years—Second Calling—in the ministry or the marketplace, there comes a time when the role you play in life and the expression of your calling may change. It is at that point you may need to discern the shape of your calling for a new phase of life. Sometimes it is by design, other times by default. You may have been downsized, "transitioned" from your job, become an empty nester, or even retired. You have entered a new phase, and now you have the opportunity to discover your Third Calling. But you will need to look inward to discern that calling for the next phase.

As Parker Palmer points out in *Let Your Life Speak*, "Vocation does not mean a goal that I pursue. It means a calling that I hear. Before I can tell my life what I want to do with it, I must listen to my life telling me who I am." [7] In our Re-Ignite Retreats, we take the time to "listen to our life" by doing life review. By looking back you gain perspective on where you have come from, which may give you clues as to where you could go from here. While you may have concluded your formal career, your calling continues to exist, and you may in fact finally be free to pursue it wholeheartedly.

Consider Tim's story. Tim enjoyed a fulfilling career in management at the Boeing Company in Everett, Washington. He later moved into an program management position at Microsoft. In his mid-50s, he began to question whether he had a long-term future there. After all, he was a history major, and the younger recruits to Microsoft came with strong backgrounds in technology. Tim was beginning to feel outpaced by the very people he supervised. The change was imminent; he just didn't know when. During this time, he began particularly noticing the needs of the poor in our city. The more he learned about Seattle's homelessness crisis, the more his passion grew to help. Tim's small group shared his concerns and organized a "Care Day" at the local high school. They invited agencies that provided services for homeless individuals and families to set up booths and offer information and give away free supplies. They enlisted over 150 volunteers to guide visitors through the maze of displays and services—and carry their bags that were filled with donated shoes, clothing and food. Care Day blessed those who came, and it planted a burning passion in Tim's heart to do more.

Tim needed to gain some perspective on his life, and what

God was calling him to do in the future. Leona and I invited Tim and his wife to join us for a week on a 53' French sailboat in the Caribbean and go through our Re-Ignite curriculum. They couldn't resist and accepted our invitation to join us on our adventure. Throughout the week, we helped them revisit their life story, define their purpose, clarify their values, discover their unique design, pursue their passion, develop a plan, and enlist a team to accomplish their vision. We encouraged them to respond to God's assignment for their Third Calling.

Within days of returning to Seattle from our sailing expedition, Tim was laid off from his job. While a bit of a shocker, Tim's experience onboard the sailboat prepared him for the transition. He was ready for what came next. He responded to an invitation to accept a position in his church serving in local outreach and community transformation. Now he gets paid to pursue his passion to care for the homeless and others in need. He is fulfilled in his Third Calling, leading the change and fueling a movement in his community to alleviate homelessness.

Students at Westmont College are offered a wide array of resources and services to help them discern their calling in life. What if those same kinds of resources were available for those in their Third Calling? What if individuals faced with a transition in their lives were able to go through the same kinds of assessments offered to college students at the front end of their career search? While many have taken such assessments during their careers, a fresh look inward can be of great benefit to prepare for the next chapter.

That is precisely what we seek to facilitate for people through our Re-Ignite events, and presentations. Just as Tim was able to revisit these themes in anticipation of a transition, leading edge Boomers would likewise benefit from "going back to school" and re-discovering what "lights their fire" in this next stage.

To that end, Leona and I, in our Third Calling, seek to challenge our peers with the message that God isn't finished with them yet. We provide resources and events that help people listen afresh to what God might be calling them to do in this stage of their lives. Through our writing, teaching, and presentations we encourage people to dig deeply to understand who they are, why there are here, and where God would have them go.

How about you? Are you facing a transition in your life that may prompt you to ask the question, "What's next?" Have you retired and find yourself in an undefined period of your life yet hungering for something meaningful to do with your remaining years? If so, we invite you to enter into this exciting journey of discovering your Third Calling.

There's a world out there just waiting for you to change it!

"When I stand before God at the end of my life, I would hope that I would not have a single bit of talent left, and could say, "I used every thing you gave me."
—Erma Bombeck

Consider: How do you define calling?

CHAPTER 3

KNOWING YOUR PURPOSE
By Richard

*"The two most important days of your life are
the day you were born and the day you find out why."*
—Mark Twain

*"The Lord will fulfill his purpose for me;
your steadfast love, O LORD, endures forever."*
—Psalm 138:8 ESV

THE BIG QUESTION: WHO ARE YOU AND WHY ARE YOU HERE?

AN OLD LEGEND TELLS OF a Jewish Rabbi who walked along the same road every day from the temple to his home. One day, being deep in thought about the events of the day, he missed a usual turn and found himself at a city gate he was unfamiliar with.

A guard yelled down from the gate, "Who are you and why are you here?"

Startled by this voice, the Rabbi looked up and asked, "Who are you?"

The guard explained that he was a guard for the King and then once again demanded an answer to his questions, "Who are you and why are you here?"

Instead of giving an answer, the Rabbi asked: "How much do

you get paid each day to stand and ask those questions to those who pass by?"

The guard was bothered by the Rabbi's odd questions, but he told him his wages.

The Rabbi then told the guard, "I will double your wages if you will come and stand outside my house and each day when I step outside, ask me those two questions."

How would your life change if someone asked you every morning, "Who are you and why are you here?"

Do you have a purpose in this stage of life? Do you know who you are and why you are here? The answers are the foundation of your Third Calling.

Every man and woman born into this world has a purpose for being alive. The challenge of life is to discover it. Purpose is defined as "the reason for which something is done or created or for which something exists. In its verb form it means to have as your intention or objective."[1]

"Here is the test to find whether your mission on earth is finished: If you're alive, it isn't."

—Richard Bach[2]

Richard Leider, executive coach, author and founder of the Inventure Group, discusses the impact of defining your life purpose in his book, *The Power of Purpose*.[3] He maintains that most people want to know that their lives have meaning—a reason to get up in the morning. As individuals grow older, he emphasizes, having a clear sense of what you are on earth to be and to do becomes increasingly important.

Purpose, then, is not a job or a role or a goal. It is the belief that our lives, our part in the whole of things, truly matter. Having a profound sense of who we are, where we came from and where we're going, we choose to believe that mattering matters.[4]

Let's take a closer look at those three elements of knowing your purpose for your Third Calling.

WHO ARE YOU?

First, to grasp true purpose in life, you first must recognize what makes each person a one-of-a-kind. The following chapters will help you take the first steps toward understanding your uniqueness—your personality, strengths, spiritual gifts, values, passions, motivational drives and dreams. Together these help clarify who you are.

Discovering my unique design has proven critical in understanding my Third Calling. For example, through various assessments I learned that I am an introvert, driven and determined to accomplish goals, analytical, gifted in administration and leadership, and motivated by opportunities where I am key and unique. I can see why I am drawn to positions of influence and leadership. In addition to my unique design, I have a clearer picture of who I am by looking at the roles I fulfill (husband, dad, grandpa, pastor) and my life experiences. One result of understanding who I am is that I can define my life purpose for my Third Calling. Through our ministry of Re-Ignite, I'm leading others in discovering their purpose.

WHERE ARE YOU FROM?

Second, if you are to know your purpose in your Third Calling, you must examine where you've come from. What events, environments and people have impacted who you are? For me, exploring my ancestral roots gave me a broader understanding of where I came from. During a trip to Sweden in June, 2012, I stood on the threshold of the countryside farmhouse where my great-grandfather had lived. In 1897, seventeen-year-old Erik Borgström left Northern Sweden for America. He eventually settled in Montana where I was born a half-century later. Standing on that porch, I gained a profound understanding of my origins.

You may not have the opportunity to track down your ancestors like I did, but you can review your own life. In Chapter 3 we will discuss some ways to do this.

My father, Rudy Bergstrom, was an avid scrapbooker. He chronicled his entire World War II flying career in a notebook. Every plane he ever flew, every student pilot he taught, every airfield where he trained was represented by a picture and detailed explanation. He also documented every trip they took to see his children and grandchildren during ten years of travel in a motor home. After he had died, I discovered a poster board of his flying history. We learned more about him as well as about ourselves. I may have inherited my dad's propensity for scrapbooking. I spent two weeks during a down time between jobs using a notebook to chronicle my life up to that point. It enabled me to see my story as a series of chapters and helped me realize there were more to be written.

WHERE ARE YOU GOING?

Third, if you are to know your purpose in the Third Calling, you must consider where you are going.

In Lewis Carroll's *Alice's Adventures in Wonderland*,[5] Alice has a profound conversation with the Cheshire Cat:

"Would you tell me, please, which way I ought to go from here?"

"That depends a good deal on where you want to get to," said the Cat.

"I don't much care where—" said Alice.

"Then it doesn't matter which way you go," said the Cat.

"—so long as I get somewhere," Alice added as an explanation.

"Oh, you're sure to do that," said the Cat, "if you only walk long enough."

In other words: "If you don't know where you're going, any

road will get you there."

For those who fail to take the time and make the effort to discover their Third Calling, retirement resembles the exchange between Alice and the Cheshire Cat. I can imagine a similar conversation taking place during an exit interview with an employee who is retiring after a long career at the same company. Many people spend time and money in financial planning for retirement, but fewer make the effort to plan a life, so any road will do. Some buy into the cultural paradigm of *retirement as leisure*. We believe we need a larger purpose for our Third Calling if we are to rise above what the media and the marketers promote as the ultimate goal of life.

Harold Koenig, M.D., author of *Purpose and Power in Retirement*, illustrates exactly what we are describing as the Third Calling. He maintains that to reach life's potential, you need to discover your calling through reflection, assessment and hard work.

> *"Retirement is the last one-third of life that no longer has the restrictions of the first two-thirds. The first one-third of life is spent growing up, obtaining an education and perhaps meeting a spouse and having children. The middle third of life is spent raising one's children and advancing in one's job or profession. Once the children are raised and leave the house and formal work life has ended, the final one-third of life begins—retirement—the last stage, the final lap, a time of unprecedented new opportunities."* [6]

Although Koenig equates the third-third of life as being a stage called retirement, it may not only describe the end of a job, it could represent an entirely new calling or career.

Ken Dychtwald, Ph.D., psychologist, gerontologist and author, emphasizes the importance of defining your purpose in this stage of life in his book, *With Purpose, Going From Success to Significance in Work and Life.*

"This can be an exciting and liberating time as you begin to think about your life not as a mission accomplished—but as a time for finding a new purpose that will give your life meaning and might just become your most joyous and nourishing time on earth." [7]

There are many well-known individuals who model for us what it means to find new or renewed purpose in this stage of life. Here are a few of them:

- Colonel Harland Sanders launched his Kentucky Fried Chicken franchise at age 65 after the interstate bypassed his restaurant where his pressure-boiled fried chicken had become a best seller.
- Winston Churchill became prime minister of England at the age of 66 and served until he was 70. Re-elected at 76 he served until he was 81 and wrote *A History of The English Speaking Peoples* at age 82.
- Benjamin Franklin played an instrumental role in drafting and signing the Declaration of Independence at age 70 and signed the Constitution of the United States at age 81.
- Ronald Reagan was elected as 40th President of the United States just a few days shy of his 70th birthday and served until he was almost 78.
- Peter Mark Roget published the first edition of his Thesaurus when he was 73 and oversaw every update until he died at age 90.
- Anna Mary Robertson didn't begin to paint until she was 76 and only did so because her hands had become so arthritic she could no longer embroider. Better known as "Grandma Moses," she turned out more than 1000 paintings in 25 years.

Consider others who discovered and know their Third Calling purpose:

- Jim and Lynn Jarman were students with us at Denver Seminary during the 1970s. They went from there to plant and pastor churches in Colorado and The Netherlands. When they returned to the U.S., they revisited their purpose for a new season of life. Upon exploring their unique design, experience, passions and calling to ministry, they clearly knew their Third Calling purpose: keep planting churches in areas that have global impact. After fund-raising, networking and training for three years, they recently moved to Stockholm, Sweden, to partner with New Life Church to coach and train millennial church planters. Their legacy will be to help launch 20-30 churches and come alongside movement leaders. In their 60s they know their purpose for their Third Calling.

- Paul and Susan retired from their day jobs a few years ago. After moving and establishing relationships in a new community, they revisited their purpose in their Third Calling. Both know they are wired and gifted for serving. While they have engaged in multiple volunteer opportunities, they also provide editing and graphics design for non-profits in their community. Thanks to them, you are reading this book with ease and clarity. They are our editors and graphic designers. Their Third Calling purpose is supporting ours.

- After taking an early retirement, Gary and Debi relocated to San Diego and purchased a home adjacent to their son's house. They know their Third

Calling purpose. As devoted grandparents, along with their son and daughter-in-law, they nurture their two grandsons.

Finally, consider a Biblical example of one who knew his Third Calling purpose—the Apostle Paul. This powerful man, who spent many years persecuting Christians, experienced a radical transformation as he traveled the road to Damascus. (Acts 9:1-19). In the days that followed, he lived out a new purpose. His life and ministry radically changed the world. Paul knew his purpose.

His story perfectly illustrates the answers to the three questions we posed at the beginning of this chapter:

- Who are you? (your identity)
- Where are you from? (your personal history)
- Where are you going? (your vision)

Paul confidently answers the question, "Who are you?" in his letter to Titus: "I am Paul. I am a servant of God and an apostle of Jesus Christ." (Titus 1:1) He found his identity in his relationship with Jesus Christ.

Paul knew all too well the answer to "Where are you from?" He had an impressive religious and educational resume and a history of successful work. He was Jewish, of the people of Israel and specifically, the tribe of Benjamin. He was a circumcised Hebrew—a Hebrew of Hebrews, he notes in Philippians 3. He was a Pharisee, a persecutor of the church and by all religious and legal standards, he was righteous and blameless. (Phil. 3: 5-6). Interestingly, in the end, it counted for nothing to him, "But whatever gain I had, I counted as loss for the sake of Christ." (Phil. 3:7 ESV)

Paul's response to "Where are you going?" was, "I have been sent to God's chosen people so that they will believe and know what is true. I do this work because then they can hope to have everlasting life." (Titus 1:1, 2 WE). He was certain of his goals and where he was headed: "Forgetting what is behind...I press on toward the goal to win the prize for which God has called me heavenward in Christ Jesus." (Philippians 3:13)

The Apostle Paul summarizes what we would call his Third Calling purpose in Philippians 3:10: It is:

"To know Christ and the power of his resurrection."

God is a God of purpose and He has a purpose for your life right now in your Third Calling. You can discover and know your purpose. Begin with asking: "Who are you?" and "Why are you here?"

"In other words, if you've got a pulse, you've got a purpose." [8]
—Darren Poke, Executive Coach

"I know the plans I have for you, says the Lord."
—Jeremiah 29:11

Consider: Do you need to discern
a new purpose for this season of life?

CHAPTER 4

STEPPING INTO YOUR STORY
by Leona

*"Life can only be understood backward; but it must be lived for-
ward."*
—Søren Kierkegaard

"Yet this I call to mind and therefore I have hope."
—Lamentations 3:21

THE SIZE AND BEAUTY OF the paintings are almost
overwhelming.

Deep within the halls of the National Gallery of Art in
Washington D.C. is a display with four walls separated by a gap
large enough for a visitor to walk through. Each wall hosts one of
the series painted by Thomas Cole entitled *The Voyage of Life*.[1] The
scenes are breathtaking.

During our visit to the gallery, Richard and I were absorbed by
this depiction of life's journey. Each painting features a traveler in a
small vessel gliding down the river of life. They are rich in color and
symbolism and elicit emotion and memories.

The first, entitled *Childhood*, depicts a smooth flowing river lined
by a lush, verdant bank. Everything is calm, warm and sheltered. The
boat is new, beautiful, intact and guided by an angel. The traveler
is a very young child whose face shows signs of awe, wonder and
innocence.

The next wall hosts the painting entitled *Youth*. The scene radiates with energy. While the landscape remains green and lush, the river becomes wider, opening to a white, billowy castle. The scene seems to represent dreams, aspirations and confidence. The traveler is a young man, who has apparently taken over the tiller and is guiding his boat. The angel is on the shore, watching.

Turning to the next wall, the painting titled *Manhood* looms in front of us. We are startled by the significant change in color, terrain and mood. The river rushes over treacherous rocks producing white water, deadly whirlpools and hazardous currents. The landscape is increasingly barren, dry and wind-torn. The traveler is a grown man; his face etched with the pain of past experience and fear for the future. His hand is no longer on the tiller; he has lost control of the boat. The angel hovers in the far distant sky.

Completing the 360-degree turn to the fourth and last painting, we gaze at *Old Age*. The traveler is an old man reaching the end of his earthly life. The river is once again calm as it broadens into a vast, eternal sea. The landscape is bare. The angel hovers close and points the way toward an opening horizon, a host of angelic beings and the hint of heaven.

We finished studying the four grand paintings. Oddly, we felt deeply disturbed. It seemed to us that the transition from adulthood to old age was abrupt and a little too hasty for our comfort. We wanted the traveler to have more time before slipping off into what seems to be his eternal destiny.

Boldly, Richard walked into the gap flanked by *Adulthood* and *Old Age* and spread his arms wide. Like Samson between the famous temple pillars, he pushed hard against the two gallery walls. "There's something missing!" he cried. "An entire stage of life is not here."

His defiant action illustrates our deep belief and what has become the foundation for Re-Ignite: Today, in the 21st century of human history, we have the opportunity for a whole new season of life. It is our Third Calling! We have sailed through childhood and are done with aspirations of youth and the accomplishments of midlife. We are at a bend in the river that opens to new possibilities! We imagine the river is lined with mature trees, ripe fruit and pink colored skies. There is no painting in the National Gallery of Art like it.

Perhaps it is ours to paint.

To be fair to Thomas Cole, when he created these masterpieces in the 1860s, life expectancy was in the mid-to-late 40s. It was common for people to go right from midlife to old age in short order.

Today? Incredibly, life expectancy has extended to late 70s for men and mid-80s for women.[2] We are seeing an entirely new stage of life come into being. As yet, no one has come up with an acceptable name for this new life stage. Some scholars call it Middlesence,[3] comparing the stage to adolescence only much latter in the life span. Others have called it Empty Nesting,[4] Encore[5] and simply, New Stage.[6] We named it Third Calling. Despite the many labels attached to this stage, Boomers are in agreement it should reflect the lengthening of midlife, not old age.

Barring disaster or disease, many of us have plenty of time for an entirely new picture. We have been given a blank canvas.

What will you paint? What will your Third Calling masterpiece look like?

Before slapping acrylics onto the empty canvas, consider depicting your personal *Voyage of Life* series. Consider stepping into your own life!

REVIEWING YOUR LIFE

Reviewing your life journey is foundational to the Re-Ignite experience and charting a course for a Third Calling. It is an invaluable spiritual and emotional exercise that sheds light on the people, life events, choices, pain and joys of our life. Looking at our past sets the stage for discovering who we are today and who we will be in the future.

Scripture reminds us of how important it is to reflect on our past and remember God's involvement in each bend of the journey:

"Bless the LORD, my soul and forget not all of his benefits."
—Psalm 103:2

"Remember the former things, those of long ago; I am God and there is no other; I am God and there is none like me."
—Isaiah 46:9

Science validates that life review is critical to our personal development, maturity and integration of life and meaning. The late Robert Butler, M.D., a respected psychiatrist, advocate for positive aging and leader in the discipline of life review, believed that considering your life can bring about a sense of peace, acceptance and resolution of conflict. The result, he maintained, is that those who intentionally review their past "have a lively capacity to live in the present." In his notable essay, *Age, Death and Life Review*, Butler suggested life review will inspire creative work "as well as a comfortable acceptance of the life cycle, the universe and the generations."[7]

Dr. Gordon MacDonald, author and Chancellor of Denver Seminary, reminds us in his book *A Resilient Life*, "We need a big picture of where we've been before we can see where we are going."[8]

Reviewing our life story is vital to envisioning our future. There are many different ways to go about it. You may write an entire autobiography that's worthy of a movie! Perhaps you will want to put together a scrapbook or a journal such as those Beth Sanders offers through LifeBio.[9] Kathryn assembled a king-size quilt that describes her life story in vibrant fabrics and stitching.

Marcia helps others share meaningful life events through "Story Ropes."[10] Sybil Towner created an entire atlas for recording and reflecting on your life journey in OneLifeMaps.[11]

It is important to spend time considering the events, themes and accomplishments of your life. Begin by picturing your life as a river, much like Cole's paintings. Identify dreams, aspirations and hopes in each stage of life. List significant people and meaningful events. Note times when you were particularly inspired, or when God "showed up."

You can get as detailed as you like; the point is that to go forward with a plan for your Third Calling, you need to see where the river started and then meandered through the years. Step into your life, see where it's been and look forward to where it is going!

"Listen to your life. See it for the fathomless mystery it is.
In the boredom and pain of it, no less than in the excitement
and gladness: touch, taste, smell your way to
the holy and hidden heart of it,
because in the last analysis all moments
are key moments and life itself is grace."[12]
— Frederick Buechner
Now and Then: A Memoir of Vocation

Here are some questions for you to reflect upon as you step into your story.

- What are some overall observations?
- Do you see any themes running through your life?
- What were the highs? What made those times so good?
- Where were times of spiritual growth? Drought?
- Where did you find evidence of God's care?
- Were there some unusual linkages or timing?
- Under what circumstances did you feel energized?

- When did you receive help to do God's work in the world?

> *"Never forget where you came from and never take your eyes off where you're heading."*
> —Unknown

> *"All the days ordained for me were written in your book before one of them came to be."*
> —Psalm 139:16

Consider: How does looking to the past influence what you will do the rest of your life?

CHAPTER 5

PURSUING YOUR PASSION
By Leona

*"That's what passion is, it's a calling...it lights you up.
And lets you know that you are exactly where you are supposed
to be, doing exactly what you are supposed to be doing."*
—Oprah

*"I was hungry and you fed me, I was thirsty and you gave me a
drink, I was homeless and you gave me a room, I was shivering and
you gave me clothes, I was sick and you stopped to visit, I was in
prison and you came to me."*
—Jesus, Matthew 25:35-36 The Message

TEXANS CLAIM THE CHILI COOK-OFF started in the
Lone Star State back in the 1950s when two chili-heads agreed to
submit their recipes for competition. Each of the chili dishes was
unique and alarmingly spicy. Local legend says that upon the first
taste, one judge ran away claiming his tongue was burned and
permanently damaged.

Since then, people around the nation have been competing
for recognition of their stew-like concoctions. Typically, all
competitors start with the standard ingredients: tomatoes, meat
and beans. What they add to the base literally makes the contest
sizzle. Everything from onions, garlic and leeks–to habanero and
ghost peppers is added to create the perfect winning recipe.

A friend entered a chili cook-off with absolutely no idea how to make the dish. Assuming if one hot chili pepper was good, then one of each variety would be superb. He went to a local farmers market and bought every type of chili pepper available, then chopped and stirred them into the pot. Not surprisingly, it set the judge's lips on fire. Our friend won an honorable mention ribbon for his innovative approach and courage to include such daring ingredients. Truly, his chili entry was full of pizzazz!

Passion is like hot peppers in a pot of chili. We all start with the basics, but passion puts the pizzazz into our life and gives our Third Calling extraordinary flavor.

Passion can be defined as what a person truly cares about. Passion underpins our dreams. It's the base of our calling. It's what lights us up and expands our heart with enthusiasm and energy. It's what energizes us; it's the force that drives us to action. Passion is the spice, when blended into a pot along with our personalities, strengths, gifts and experience that can literally blow the top off!

How do you discover and pursue your passion in this season of life?

DISCOVERING YOUR PASSION

You may be very clear about your life's passion. It might be a social cause, a group of people, a project, or perhaps an injustice. You know what it is because it's what you think about constantly. It stirs your soul, gets you out of bed in the morning and takes you into the world.

Or, you may not be so certain. In fact, you aren't sure there are any hot peppers in the chili. The fire has died down for many reasons. We will discuss that later, but for now, let's work at spicing things up.

How do you discover your passion? Begin by answering the following questions:

1. How would you use a gift of a million dollars if it

had to be given away or designated for a cause, issue or problem?

Ok, let's start with $50,000. Every year for a decade, Encore. org,[1] a national organization headquartered in San Francisco, has awarded the Purpose Prize to individuals who model their theme: "Second Acts for the Greater Good." Funded by contributors such as the John Templeton Foundation, Eisner Foundation and MetLife, Encore has awarded prize monies to over 500 social entrepreneurs, all over the age of 60.

The broad range of program innovation is impressive and, without exception, each one meets a pressing social need. Equally inspiring is the passion that motivates every prize nominee and recipient.

Reverend Belle Mickelson is a recent Purpose Prize honoree. She was deeply touched by the rising rates of depression and suicide in Alaska, particularly in small, remote villages. Believing music and the arts could bring hope and intergenerational connection, Belle founded *Dancing with the Spirit*. At age 67, she travels across interior Alaska with fiddlers and volunteer teachers in tow. Communities come together to sing, dance, laugh and celebrate their own homegrown music. Currently, she is developing suicide prevention materials in addition to the music program.

Another Purpose Prize recipient is Jamal Joseph. He grew up in the Bronx and at age 15 joined the Black Panther party. While in prison because of his involvement with the Black Panthers, he took a mentor's advice to "not serve time, but let time serve him." He received two college degrees and also started a drama group in the prison A few years ago, while in his early 60s, he witnessed increasing violence and despair ripping apart the youth in his community. He decided to do something about it.

He founded IMPACT, a repertory theater located in Harlem, designed to give troubled youth a safe place to participate in theater, art and dancing. Over 1,500 teens have participated in the program and countless lives have been touched through community workshops and events. In a taped interview, Jamal Joseph said, "I realized this was not a hobby, this was a mission." Joseph is living out his passion.

These Purpose Prize winners initiated programs before they were ever recognized by Encore or given award money. They had a passion for solving problems and meeting needs. I'm pretending to offer you a million dollars to go and meet a need. What will you do with it?

2. What makes your blood boil?

Several years ago we convinced Paula to go on a short-term mission trip with us to Nicaragua. Recently retired from teaching, Paula was perplexed about her purpose in life and uncertain why she was going on this particular trip to Nicaragua. During the trip we visited the La Chureca garbage dump in Managua. Feeling overwhelmed after seeing a school in the midst of the stench and ugliness of a dump, Paula settled into the back seat of our air-conditioned van, ready to go home. Just as we were preparing to leave, a young girl with a beautiful smile pressed her nose to the side window and waved goodbye. Paula looked into those sad eyes and her heart was deeply moved.

Several months later we received a message that this little girl with the sweet smile had died from complications of HIV/AIDS. She contracted the disease through sexual contact with the garbage truck drivers. She had been prostituted to dump truck drivers in exchange for them leaving the best, resalable garbage near her family's shack. Paula's blood boiled. Looking into the eyes of a vulnerable child who had been sold was absolutely unbearable. Paula was never the same. Before long, she was the leader of a non-profit organization determined to fight human trafficking around the world.

The little girl with the big smile instilled passion in others to fight human trafficking. Years after our encounter with her in the Nicaraguan dump, we were introduced to Brad Corrigan, a musician from Denver. He met this same little girl while on a mission trip in 2006 and had developed a special relationship with her. He told us her name was Ileana. He was so moved by her life, death—and faith in Jesus—he decided to share her story as far and wide as possible. Through his non-profit organization, Love Light + Melody, Brad is producing a documentary titled *Ileana's Smile*.[2] He hopes to ignite passion in others' hearts to halt this injustice.

3. What makes you cry?

A distinguished, fashionably dressed businesswoman raised her hand during one of our Re-Ignite Retreats. "Do you want to know what makes me cry?" she asked. "I'll tell you." Tears started filling her eyes. "It's when I see homeless people unable to feed their dogs." Choked up, she was unable to go on with her explanation. Several days later I received an email from her. Attached was a picture of a plastic baggie filled with dog biscuits, a gift card for pet food and a handwritten note. "After leaving the retreat I realized I was passionate about this," she wrote. "I had an idea of how I could help. I'm putting these gift baggies together and taking them to people with homeless pets."

4. What makes you slam your fist on the table and say, "Someone should do something about this?"

I pounded the table and said something similar when Leila told me about the plight of elderly people in her country. She was sent by the government of Moldova to study at the University of Washington as a Herbert Hoover Graduate Fellow. Knowing I had spent my career in developing programs for older people, she wanted to talk about the systems of care provided in the U.S. In the course of the conversation, she told me that elders in her country had little to eat and some were actually starving. My heart broke. I shed tears. I said, "Someone ought to do something about that!" Before we parted, I took Leila's hand in mine and said something that changed my life. "Leila, someday I will help you feed your old people."

My passion came into focus.

I have always had a passion for those living a long time. I've developed programs to protect and enhance the integrity of old age. I've dedicated my life to serving elders in my community. Moldova's old women called to me and I knew, without a doubt, that the "someone" who should do something—was me! I went to Moldova and along with several others, helped support an elder lunch program provided by Bethany Church in Chisinau. Today seniors at CRISTA Senior Living in Seattle where I worked at the time of my visit to Moldova, continue to send money every month to help feed their peers in another country. Pounding my fist helped me realize just how much I cared about older people in another country as well as in my community.

What makes your blood boil? What do you care about? What makes you cry? What should you do something about?

That's your passion.

WHOM WERE YOU MEANT TO SERVE?

I was meant to serve older people. I am called to serve my peers, the Boomers, who will never be "older" but who may live a long time. I am passionate about challenging people to find their Third Calling.

The Third Calling is always about making the world a better place. It's about finding a mission that only you can follow; a purpose only you can fulfill.

"Every mission implies that someone will be helped. A nation will be freed, a bird will be returned to its nest again, a child will have a new image of what parental love can be.

Whom were you sent here to help?"

—Laurie Beth Jones, *The Path* [3]

There are many causes, people or groups that you may serve in your Third Calling. Here's a limited list. Select two or three that evoke a passionate response from your heart and soul. If you cannot find yours, add it to the list.

Abortion AIDS Substance abuse Orphans Education

Children Marriages Mental Health Homelessness

Christians Elderly Missions Environment Animals

Literacy Justice Climate Human Trafficking Politics

Healthcare Travel Arts Technology Addictions

Divorced LGBT Prisoners Disability Widowed

Sick/dying Victims of Abuse Economy The Poor

Adults Youth Singles

Examine the reasons for your passion for those causes, people or groups.

As you review your life, you may note frequent interactions with a group or cause. For me, I can look at my life story and see how I was naturally drawn to older people. Elders contributed to my understanding of life, told me their stories, mentored and encouraged me. It is not surprising that I am passionate about long life and finding purpose in it.

Look for times in your life experiences when you were particularly energized while serving a group or cause. Did you come alive when you served soup at a center for homeless people? Did you find unexplainable joy when you sat with a friend at the bedside of her dying mother? Did you find satisfaction leading a team to clean a park on Earth Day? What energizes you?

Do you share common experiences with others that connect you? Perhaps you know what it is like to decide to refuse an abortion, or remain single or join a political protest. Passion comes from experience. Living your passion connects your experience to others and helps meet a need.

Sometimes life's events disconnect us from our passion. We get distracted. We have to provide for our families. We are thrust into caregiving for our parents or grandchildren. There are many reasons why we can become disconnected from that which we are called to serve. That's why our Third Calling is a gift!

IGNITE YOUR PASSION

Today is the day to begin lighting the fire of your passion and Third Calling! What would you do, if there were no limits, to serve the cause, people or groups you've identified?

Here's how to fan the flame:

- Seek God's heart. What concerns Him? Search scriptures that tell us what God cares about. (read Micah 6:8, John 4:35, Deut. 15:11, Luke 15:32)
- Revisit a time when you knew this cause, people or group in a way that moved you deeply. What did you focus on or think about during earlier stages of your life?
- Explore organizations, ministries, non-profit groups and other people who are doing things to serve the people you care about.
- Take responsibility for igniting your passion. Do something every day that enlarges your vision and makes you more aware of the need.
- Do something to move forward! Volunteer at a homeless shelter. Read a story at the library's toddler hour or make art every day. Do something!
- Publicly declare your passion and intentions.

By the way, today chili cook-offs have become more than recipe contests. Through them, non-profit and service organizations fulfill their calling and mission by raising millions of dollars every year. In a sense, chili cook-offs are changing the world.

"If you can't figure out your purpose, figure out your passion.
For your passion will lead you right into your purpose."
—Bishop T.D. Jakes

Consider: What is one thing you could do today to serve the people or cause you care deeply about?

CHAPTER 6
AWAKENING YOUR DREAMS
By Leona

"You are never too old to set another goal or to dream a new dream."
—C.S. Lewis

"Hope deferred makes the heart sick,
but a dream fulfilled is a tree of life."
—Proverbs 13:12, NLT

YOUNG RAPUNZEL HAD A DREAM. All of her life she dreamed of seeing the floating lanterns that were launched once every year across the skies of the Kingdom. The desire burned furiously in her heart, but she was trapped, actually imprisoned, in a tower by an evil woman pretending to be her mother.[1]

This Brothers Grimm fairy tale is a story of a young maiden with a dream, which became a plan (that, of course, includes a dashing young man) and eventually a glorious reality. It's the stuff movies are made of, so not surprisingly, in 2010 Disney released the movie, *Tangled*.[2] It is the picture of how a dream awakens.

One scene in the movie says it best. Rapunzel and her reluctant liberator, Flynn Rider, enter the Snuggly Duckling Pub filled with questionable ghouls and characters. Frustrated with the obstacles they presented to pursuing her dream, Rapunzel stands on the table and yells,

"All right people! Haven't you ever had a *dream*?"

The grubby atmosphere is transformed as one-by-one, each ghoul sheds his gruff exterior and not only describes his dream but sings about it!

This question is important to ask as you discover your Third Calling. Have you ever had a dream?

FROM DREAM TO VISION TO REALITY

I have dreams—lots of them. Some envision great things for my life, my family, things I want to see and experience and places I want to live.

Professionally, I've had some big dreams, most of them flowing out of my passion to see long life that is full of joy, of purpose and valued by our culture.

While serving as the Director of the Senior Health Department at a local hospital, I began to recognize a dream. In my ideal world, I wanted to assure that all older people had access to excellent health care, vibrant social interaction and opportunities for lifelong learning and productivity.

My dream, when awakened, became a vision. I pictured a one-stop center where individuals could: receive specialized health care provided by a trained geriatrician, obtain appropriate interventions by a social worker, be guided toward healthier living by a nutritionist/dietician, find spiritual guidance and assurance by a chaplain and engage in educational opportunities. And, of course, have a place to exercise in a state-of-the-art wellness center!

The vision required a well-developed strategy to become a reality. The plan included research, endless presentations to convince hospital leadership of the necessity for such a clinic, fundraising and intense team building. It took two years for a multi-disciplinary team to plan, develop and build the Center for Senior Health.

On July 10, 1999, dignitaries from throughout the community passed through a helium balloon arch and entered a beautiful center complete with a clinic, classrooms and sparkling new treadmills. We had overcome obstacles, opposition and exhausting challenges. Nelson Mandela's famous quote: "It always seems impossible until it's done," described my feelings exactly. My dream cost me a lot, but the thrill of seeing it become a vision and then reality, was indescribably fulfilling.

Will and Rebecca Stout had a dream. They wanted to help people who had been hurt or depleted while working in ministry. The extraordinary part of their dream was to take those bleeding warriors on a sailboat and help them experience the adventure and healing that the Caribbean Sea would offer. It was a huge dream that became a vision when they began to make a plan.

Richard and I first met Will and Rebecca during a Re-Ignite Retreat planning team meeting. After discussing the logistics of hosting the event in their church, Will said, "We just have to talk to you guys!" Later in the week we had dinner and they shared their BHAG (big hairy audacious goal) with us. It sounded pretty exotic and a little crazy. We suggested they go through the Re-Ignite Retreat and see if they sensed God's leading to proceed.

They attended, explored their unique design and calling, sought God's leading and went forward to map out a radical, dream-chasing, God-inspired vision. They disposed of many possessions, sold their house, quit their jobs and took delivery of their dream sailboat, which was moored in a harbor on the island of Curacao. They established and launched *Catch the Wind Sailing Ministries.*[3] Today they live aboard the Anni Bea True, sail the seas and minister to people in need of TLC and a bit of excitement.

Their dream became a vision; their vision became a reality.

They are, in every meaning of the word, charting a new course.

EVERYONE HAS THE RIGHT TO DREAM

During a Re-Ignite Retreat reunion, one participant shared a tremendous insight. In the course of the weekend, she identified some of the dreams and hopes she had in earlier years. Life, as it often does, had gotten in the way of her pursuing some of those passions and goals. So had her church experience. Somewhere along the line, she internalized a message that she should squelch imagination, creativity and the pursuit of those things that might appear self-seeking.

Her comment was simple and startling: "I didn't know it was okay to dream."

Not only is it okay, it is to be expected! Our Creator places dreams deep within our hearts. Our responsibility is to turn them into a vision and follow a plan.

How do you turn your dream into reality?

1. Identify your dream. What is the ideal that you want to experience or see come to fruition? Is it a project, a building or a concept?
2. Seek God's inspiration and imagination.
3. Create a vision for the future. What would it look like if your dream was fulfilled?
4. Develop a strategy to make your vision a reality. Include your timeline, budget and potential partners.
5. Nurture your dream and vision with prayer.
6. Give it time.

"Never give up on a dream just because of the time
it will take to accomplish it. The time will pass anyway."
—Earl Nightingale

OUR DREAM FOR RE-IGNITE

Richard and I have a dream to see our generation living full and purposeful lives. Our desire comes from our life experience, passions and values. We want to influence others to make their lives count and leave the world a better place.

Our dream became a vision when we began developing the Re-Ignite ministry process. The strategy included writing curriculum, creating a website and developing a retreat and speaking ministry. We are seeing that become a reality. The pinnacle of the vision is to write a book that will influence others and inspire them to live with passion and purpose. Transforming that dream into a vision requires a strategy for determining content, obtaining production assistance and choosing the publishing strategy.

If you are reading this, then our dream is a reality!

By the way, in the end Rapunzel escaped her tower, ran away with her hero and saw the soaring lighted lanterns. In the process, she discovered she was a princess. Ah, dreams, they can come true.

Now, can we talk about my house on the beach?

> *"The future belongs to those who believe
> in the beauty of their dreams."*
> —Eleanor Roosevelt

Consider: Make a sketch of what your fulfilled dream could look like.

PART TWO:

YOU WERE MEANT FOR THIS

CHAPTER 7
CLARIFYING YOUR VALUES
By Leona

"Values become your destiny."
—Mahatma Gandhi

"Therefore, everyone who hears these words of mine and puts them into practice is like a wise man who built his house on a rock."
—Matthew 7:24

DOODLING. THAT'S ALL HE WAS doing. Drawing a little face with a big smile to counteract the gloom and doom he was feeling watching the evening news. Bert named him "Jake" and hung him on his apartment wall.

That was the beginning of what is now a vast retail industry. T-shirts, beach bags, dog tags, coffee mugs, stationery, home decorations and tire covers—anything that can display words and stick-figure art—are products that share the Jacobs brothers' worldview of optimism and hope. Their message is based on a core belief that life is good.

The story of Bert and John Jacobs' company, Life is Good,[1] and its rapid rise to success and universal recognition, is fascinating. Their efforts took them from selling their first 48 custom-designed T-shirts from the back of their van to operating a $100 million dollar international business. They believe in and distribute hope. Their products, work environment and profits all support their values. What's more, they help millions of people declare their personal values through wearing T-shirts with pictures of little stick-figures doing whatever it is they consider important. My personal favorite is the design of a couple driving a red convertible.

The Life is Good story is profound in many ways. Certainly, the tale of two charming college students making good is irresistible. Even more profound is the message of how life-giving it is for you to know what matters and then make choices and decisions accordingly.

What message would you wear? What do you believe in that makes life good? What is important to you?

Defining what matters to you is vital to determine your Third Calling.

VALUES: WHAT REALLY MATTERS

Before answering the question of what truly matters, it is important to define what is meant by the word "values."

Values are those things you believe important in the way you live and work. They are principles or standards that are considered worthwhile and desirable. Naturally, when actions match values, you feel satisfied, content, in balance and in alignment. Life is good, even if difficult (think living justly in an evil world.) But when action and behaviors do not align with values, life feels amiss, wrong, disconnected.

After developing the Re-Ignite curriculum and facilitating numerous retreats and events, we came face-to-face with what it means to live according to our own values. During an exercise where we ask participants to prioritize their values, Richard agonized over his response to the question, "For each of the values you prize the most, how much are you experiencing in your current life or job?" He realized the extent of the chasm between what he valued and how he was living. He valued creativity, independence and influence, but his full-time church staff position demanded his actions display conformity, organization, compliance and authority. He recognized why he was exhausted, frustrated and felt trapped. When asked, "What may need to change to align your life, job, or career with your values?" He responded: "I need to sell my house, quit my job and return to my true calling."

One year later, we had sold our house, Richard quit his job and we were devoting full-time efforts to the development of our Re-Ignite Ministry. When action and behaviors do not align with values, life feels amiss, wrong, disconnected. We realigned our life to match our values. We were ready to engage our Third Calling!

VALUES ARE THE FOUNDATION FOR DETERMINING NEW DIRECTIONS

> *"If you want to know about your values,*
> *recall the moments you want to re-live."*
> —Tasneed Hameed

When you discern your core values, they become the foundation for making decisions, setting priorities and defining boundaries. You can begin to answer questions like: Should I start my own business? Move closer to the family? Travel a new path?

While priorities change in different seasons, core values typically remain stable throughout our lives. Before you identify your core values, stop to review your life story. Look back over your experiences, decisions and choices you have made. What values drove those decisions?

Identify times when you were most happy. Why? What were you doing? When were you the most proud? Why? What had you accomplished? When did you feel fulfilled? Why did the experience give you meaning and satisfaction?

Most of us have "shoulds" playing in our minds—those things society and culture elevate or impose upon us as values, some more important than others. Most of us also experience parental values that still hover over us. Many of us identify our religious beliefs or standards as core values. While all of these are noteworthy, it is critical to stand back and recognize what is important to you.

We want to help you to clarify your values. The following list of values are commonly held by individuals living in modern western societies. Add any values you consider missing. Now circle ten words that are most important to you.

COMMON VALUES

Authenticity	Family	Love
Achievement	Fitness	Loyalty
Adventure	Friendships	Optimism
Authority	Fun	Nature
Balance	Gratitude	Recognition
Beauty	Happiness	Responsibility
Compassion	Harmony	Security
Challenge	Honesty	Service
Compassion	Humor	Simplicity
Competency	Influence	Stability
Control	Integrity	Success
Courage	Justice	Tolerance
Creativity	Knowledge	Wealth
Faith	Learning	Wisdom

Next, cross out one at a time to prioritize your top five values. This step may be the most difficult because you'll have to look deep inside yourself. It is also the most important step, because, when you make decisions about what your Third Calling will be, you must choose between solutions that may satisfy different values. At this point you must know which value is more important to you.

To help you prioritize, it will help to visualize a situation where you have to make a decision or choice. For example, when you compare the values of loyalty and achievement, imagine that you must decide whether to continue working in a company owned by your best friend or leave and accept a higher-level leadership position somewhere else.

Keep working through the list until you can identify one value that supersedes all of them.

Life is Good founders, Bert and John Jacobs, identified their top ten values. Those became the pillars upon which their entire lives and business are based. Their top ten: simplicity, humor, gratitude, fun, compassion, creativity, authenticity, love, openness and courage. If you were to press them for their number one core value, they would summarize the top ten into one word: optimism. It is optimism that fuels creativity and the other values they feel are so important.

DECIDING WHAT MATTERS WILL INFLUENCE YOUR FUTURE

Anna was an educator. She loved teaching and delighted in watching students learn and achieve their goals. Following the birth of her second child, she took several months off. She never returned to the school or her position as a fifth-grade teacher. During maternity leave, her newborn child died of SIDS. As Anna slowly reassembled the pieces of her life, she realized she valued her children and family above all. Willing to sacrifice financial security and position, she opted to become a stay-at-home mom. When her third child was born, she chose to return to teaching, this time as a home-school educator.

Her children have left home and are now pursuing advanced degrees. Anna admits she is a bit lost in this season of her life. She gave up her profession for what she valued, for what mattered to her. No longer certified to teach, the decision made years ago has influenced her future, her now. She is seeking to discover her Third Calling.

Patrick and Sally identified "adventure" and "family" as core values. They took an early retirement, purchased a 35' motor home and went on the road. They traveled to each of their adult children's homes, parked in their driveways for six weeks at a time and for ten years and spent quality time with their grandchildren. Their core values led to radical decisions that influenced their future and defined their Third Calling.

Bill and Betty both value financial security and stability. While many of their peers changed jobs, moved to new houses and took luxurious vacations, Bill and Betty stayed steady, saved diligently, paid off their mortgage and retired right on schedule with the funds to last for decades. Their stability is built on the result of living their core values. Now they are asking, "What's next?" Interestingly, they also share the core values of generosity and compassion. Theirs is going to be a fascinating Third Calling.

DECIDING WHAT MATTERS WILL IMPACT OTHERS

We do not live in a vacuum. Our value-driven actions will always affect others.

Don and Pat determined they valued friendship, influence and faith. They wanted to be available to their neighbors and extend love and hearty conversation. They decided to remodel their detached garage and turn it into a gathering place. They call it their *Cowboy Kitchen*. Pat starts nearly every day by baking pastries and making coffee. Don puts out the welcome flag and the neighbors know it's okay to come and hang out for a while. Chats seem random, but Pat and Don are conscious of the opportunities to share their faith. They decided what matters and it impacts others.

During our Re-Ignite Retreats, we show a clip from the movie, *Schindler's List*.[2] It features Oskar Schindler, a wealthy businessman living in Poland. He was also a member of the Nazi party and for some time worked as a spy for the Third Reich. He valued and pursued prosperity and status. That is until he realized the full extent his government's intention to eliminate the entire Jewish race.

He was overwhelmed by his core belief that human life has immeasurable value. He proceeded to spend his entire fortune in bribing SS officers to prevent the execution of his Jewish workers. In so doing, Schindler saved nearly 1200 Jewish lives. He decided what mattered and it deeply impacted individual lives—and history, for that matter.

The story of Bert and John Jacobs (Life is Good) delivering hope to their little neighborhood through printed T-shirts is heart-warming. They cared about the human spirit then and they still do today. In valuing optimism and declaring, "Life is Good," they began receiving letters from children whose lives were not so good.

Deeply touched by the needs of children suffering from trauma, they partnered with a child relief agency and formed the Life is Good Foundation.[3] Their company donates 10% of its profits to the Foundation. They also sponsor fund-raising events and provide scholarships and training for childcare workers. Bert and John Jacobs believe life should be good for all children. Their core value, to share optimism, deeply impacts others.

> *"It's not hard to make decisions once*
> *you know what your values are."*
> —Roy Disney

Consider: Design your own Life is Good T-shirt. What drawing and message would you put on it?

CHAPTER 8

DISCOVERING YOUR DESIGN
By Richard

"Be yourself. Everyone else is already taken."
—Oscar Wilde

"I am fearfully and wonderfully made."
—Psalm 139

AFTER TWO YEARS OF PRIVATE lessons, hours of required practice and several recitals, our 8-year-old daughter confidently informed us she no longer wanted to play the piano. "I'm just not wired for it," she alleged. She went on to excel in gymnastics and athletics, eventually graduating with a Master's degree in kinesiology and exercise. As a child, Lynnea understood something that many miss for their entire lives: each one of us is uniquely and distinctively designed.

Rick Warren, in his best-selling book, *Purpose Driven Life*, explains: "We don't realize how truly unique each of us is. DNA molecules can unite in an infinite number of ways. The number is 10 to the 2,400,000,000th power. That number is the likelihood that you'd ever find somebody just like you. If you were to write out that number with each zero being one inch wide, you'd need a strip of paper 37,000 miles long! Your uniqueness is a scientific fact of life. When God made you, he broke the mold. There never has been and never will be, anybody exactly like you."[1]

Why is this an important concept for us to grasp? Could it be we are designed, wired—yes, created—for a purpose? For our Third Calling?

Rosemarie and Wally are both college professors with earned Ph.D.s, his in theology and hers in intercultural studies.

Wally has taught in universities for nearly 30 years, so you would think they might consider retirement and a life of leisure. Instead, they packed their downsized belongings and moved to Southeast Asia. There they teach in six universities, support local Christians and help plant new churches. When asked why they would give up the comforts of retirement to go on this daring mission, Rosemarie answered, "We were created to do this."

Created? Yes. Both have personalities, strengths, gifts, values and passions that together form uniquely designed individuals, created for the challenge of this particular work in a foreign land. They are created for their Third Calling.

In the 2007 comedy, *The Nanny Diaries*, Annie Braddock (played by Scarlett Johanssen) interviews for a position in a financial analyst training program in a large New York firm. The kind and self-assured interviewer asks her first question: "Why don't you tell me in your own words, Who exactly is Annie Braddock?" Smiling confidently, Annie responds, "Well, that certainly is an easy enough question—well, um well—Annie Braddock is—Annie Braddock is a kind—um, well—I have no idea." Without an answer, she runs out of the interview and back onto the street. The audience hears her asking herself, "Who am I? That's not exactly a trick question. Sure, I know the basic stuff—age, socioeconomic status—but, I have absolutely no idea who I am!"[2]

Who are you? What are you wired to be and to do? Are you ready to embrace those things that make you unique? In this chapter, we will discuss four components that comprise your unique design: personality, strengths, spiritual gifting and motivations.

PERSONALITY

How would you define personality?

Most of us would describe personality as the essence of a person, how you behave, or your unique characteristics or qualities.

Charles M. Schwab, a famous late-19th-century American businessman, said it well: "Personality is to a man what perfume is to a flower."

We may have some idea what our personalities are like, yet, no matter our level of self-awareness, we can find ourselves taking one or more of the personality assessments that float across our Facebook pages every day. We can see what kind of animal or bird we resemble, what color describes us, which celebrity we behave like, or which car depicts our essence. These light-hearted tests may not be scientifically reliable, but we do enjoy catching a glimpse into how we tick.

There is much that contributes to our personality including heredity, brain development, physical characteristics and a cultural and social environment. As we discover our Third Calling, it is important to understand our unique personalities and how we behave.

There are excellent tests and assessments that can help you gain more self-awareness. One of our favorites is the DISC Personality Profile. Created in 1928 by Dr. William Marston, psychiatrist, the assessment provides insights into how individuals think, act and interact. The profile measures four behavioral traits: (D) dominance, (I) influence, (S) steadiness and (C) conscientiousness. PeopleKeys,[3] an organization that offers personality assessments and training for businesses and corporations, describes the DISC traits:

- Dominant (D)
  Direct, outspoken, results-oriented, a leader, problem-solver
- Influencing (I)
  Friendly, outgoing, talkative, optimistic, the life of the party, people-oriented
- Steady (S)
  Team player, stable, consistent, maintains the

status quo, peacemaker, family-oriented, patient
- Compliant (C)
  Logical, organized, data-driven, methodical, perfectionist, detail-oriented

PeopleKeys offers a free online DISC assessment to discover your personality style.[4] The Meyers-Briggs Temperament Inventory and the Kiersey Bates Temperament Sorter stand out among other inventory assessments and can give you great insights into your personality style. Free assessments are available on the internet.

STRENGTHS

Dr. Donald O. Clifton, an American psychologist, is known as the Father of Strengths-based Psychology. He coined an entirely new language for self-understanding when he introduced the concept of defining and developing your strengths rather than your weaknesses. Based upon 40 years of studying and interviewing thousands of individuals, he described 34 common talent themes. He created Strengths Finder, an assessment tool that millions of people around the world have taken. Today, Strengths Finder is a part of Gallup, a research-based, international, management consulting company.

The Strengths Finder report identifies your dominant themes in order of strength. Most people choose to focus on the top five themes and work to strengthen them. Clifton defines strength as—"the ability to provide consistent, near-perfect performance in a given activity."[5] To become strong, you must take what is natural (talent) and add knowledge and skill to make it a strength.

It's easy to picture muscles getting stronger. We know it takes work. Leona had the privilege of working with faculty at Western Washington University several years ago when they were researching the impact weight-bearing exercise had on developing bone and muscle mass in elderly women. The improvement gained as a result of the strengthening exercises was astounding. In the same way, we can exercise our natural talents, so they are our greatest strengths and our gifts to the world.

Our friend, Elisa, has a natural talent for creating order. Even as a child, she would organize everything she could find—toys in crates, shoes in boxes, combs and barrettes neatly arranged in drawers. She always thought she might be a little weird because she was just naturally talented at organizing. As a midlife adult, Elisa attended a Re-Ignite Retreat and as part of the process took the Strengths Finder assessment. She discovered she had natural talents for organizing and arranging things for maximum productivity. She also scored high in creating order and in wanting to make what is good become great.

Elisa began celebrating her natural talents and started exercising them. She took classes and learned how to launch a business. Today she is president of her company, How2Organize and just released her first book, *Calming Your Chaos*.[6] Discovering how she is uniquely designed was the key to following her Third Calling.

You may formally take a Gallup Strengths Finder[7] assessment, or simply begin listing what you perceive are your natural talents. The key is to invest time and energy in the things you do well naturally and develop them into something extraordinary.

> *"Master your strengths. Outsource your weaknesses."*
> —Ryan Kahn, Career Coach

MOTIVATIONS

Why do you do what you do? What gives you joy? Where is the frustration in your job, ministry or life?

Understanding what "gets you up in the morning" is a core piece of discovering your Third Calling. Your activity in the next season of life will be fresh and inspiring if you do what motivates you!

In Re-Ignite, we offer the MCORE[8] assessment to discover your motivational pattern. MCORE utilizes narrative, the telling of your stories of accomplishment and satisfaction, to determine three top motivational patterns in your life.

A more extensive assessment is SIMA[9] (The System for Identifying Motivated Abilities), based on an in-depth interview, narratives and intense analysis and coaching.

Identifying motivations is life changing. Leona and I share one motivational theme: Experience the Ideal. According to the MCORE description: "You are motivated to give concrete expression to certain concepts, visions or values that are important to you. You want to live out your ideas and ideals and to measure up to a self-image or role you adopt or are cast in. The process of striving to realize these ideals may be what gives you satisfaction and pleasure."

Understanding our motivation in this way has encouraged us to write this book—together! We are driven by our core motivation to research, write and present this material to help you discover your Third Calling. It is certainly foundational to ours.

SPIRITUAL GIFTING

There are many components to our uniqueness. We've talked about personality, strengths and motivations—the combination makes each of us distinctive, exceptional—and one of a kind.

Christians have another element to their uniqueness— spiritual gifting. You've got the power to fulfill your Third Calling because God himself provides it.

Both the Old and New Testaments of the Bible list gifts that God imparts to us to impact the world. They include preaching, teaching, mercy, administration, leadership, giving, faith, service and wisdom and more.

You may want to take a spiritual gifts assessment [10] or inventory to help you identify what God has given you supernatural power to do.

Erik and Lari just became grandparents. They are in their 50s and both work full-time in administrative and executive positions. They are wired to tend to details and manage projects. Their personalities are outgoing and engaging—they are both true extroverts. Motivated by meeting needs and encouraging others, they are discovering a new purpose for their Third Calling—hospitality. Together they are serving delectable meals and banquets for their church and community. They consistently open their home to friends, family and neighbors. Their culinary expertise is phenomenal; their love is supernatural. Their Third Calling is all about service. Not to mention, they make an incredible BBQ sauce.

YOU ARE ONE OF A KIND

You are uniquely designed with a distinctive personality, talents and strengths, motivations and spiritual gifts! It is mind-boggling to consider there are no two people alike in all of the history of the universe.

You are equipped for your Third Calling.

Celebrate.

Live fully.

Change the world!

Consider: Describe a personal accomplishment for which you were proud and felt satisfaction and joy.

CHAPTER 9
CULTIVATING YOUR CREATIVITY
By Leona and Richard

"Those who do not think outside the box are easily contained."
—Nicolas Manetta

*"For everything God created is good and nothing is to be rejected
if it is received with thanksgiving."*
—I Timothy 4:4

DEFINING CREATIVITY—Leona

"WHITTLING," HE CALLED IT. MY grandpa would take out his pocketknife, pick up a piece of leftover building scrap and within a few hushed moments, a little wooden man emerged. I always assumed whittling was a way for him to pass the time, perhaps even his hobby. I didn't fully grasp the fact that Grandpa was cultivating his creativity.

Similarly, I misjudged the intent of the hundreds of clubs and classes offered at The Villages, a large retirement community in Florida. Ceramics, painting, quilting, scrapbooking, model cars, flower arranging, writing and crocheting classes attract hundreds of participants every day. Far from just whittling away the hours, they are cultivating creativity.

Scientific studies prove that something unique happens to the brain as it ages. The late Gene Cohen, M.D., Ph.D., author of *The Creative Age* states, "Studies of aging are showing that the potential for creative expression in the second half of life is not the exception but the rule. Creative expression occurs not despite aging, but because of aging."[1]

Grandpa's woodchip masterpieces were not by-products of his boredom; rather they were manifestations of a mature mind coming alive with imagination, inspiration and originality.

Creativity is not limited to expression through the arts; it is a requirement in all spheres of our lives. Creativity unlocks doors to new possibilities, novel solutions and innovative approaches. Well-known author, toy-maker and creativity consultant, Roger Von Oechs, describes creativity as a "whack on the side of the head."[2] He believes by looking at problems and opportunities in new and perhaps outlandish ways, we can discover solutions and ideas that go beyond our imagination.

Cultivating your creativity is an essential to embarking on the journey of your Third Calling.

"Creativity is a lot like looking at the world through a kaleidoscope.
You look at a set of elements, the same ones everyone else sees,
but then reassemble those floating bits and pieces
into an enticing new possibility."
—Rosabeth Moss Kanter

DISCOVERING AND CULTIVATING MY CREATIVE SIDE—Richard

After just one year working in a para-church ministry in Southern California, I made a change and joined another organization. We headed back to our home in Bellingham, Washington. It was our second cross-country move in only twelve months. The entire experience was an expensive and frustrating lesson in understanding the corporate culture of even Christian organizations. Before joining the staff of the second organization, I was asked to take the DISC assessment.

(See Chapter 8 for more about DISC). My profile results described my personality as High D—dominant, driven and determined. However, when combined with the secondary theme "C" I fit, what DISC calls, the *Creative Pattern*. The description reads: "Those with the 'creative pattern' are aggressive, determined leaders who infuse energy and meaning into lifeless systems. They set the pace in developing new and unusual ideas. Creative persons are detailed and meticulous leaders who are blunt and critical." Interestingly, this particular version of DISC also provided a comparison to a Biblical character. Had the Apostle Paul taken the DISC assessment, he most likely would have also been described a High D/Complementary C; the *Creative Pattern*. Paul was driven to accomplish the arduous mission of spreading the gospel throughout the known world, challenging and breathing new life into old religious systems and calling believers to total commitment.

Light bulbs went on as I came to understand why the previous year with my former organization was so frustrating. As I dug deeper into the DISC assessment, I realized my desire to influence others by "setting a pace in developing systems; task or project completion," and my "value to an organization was as an initiator or designer of changes." (DISC) Because I was not allowed opportunities to suggest creative ways of doing things in the organization and was simply expected to implement their agenda, I jumped ship and joined another group that would allow me greater freedom. Even then, I found the parameters too constricting for my creative spirit and eventually launched my own organization. (See Chapter 10, "Unleashing Your Inner Entrepreneur.")

I've seen this pattern expressed throughout my life. I seem to be determined to discover creative and innovative approaches to challenges, problems and opportunities.

Here are some personal examples:

- Determined to develop a unique talent and ministry, I learned ventriloquism while in high school and performed for a variety of events.
- Determined to challenge the dominant paradigm of a "successful" church, I created an instructional, social simulation board game called SUPERCHURCH. It became the basis for my doctoral project.
- Determined to help ministry leaders in strategic planning, I developed a unique assessment tool called *The Church Sets Sail*. I used graphics of sailboats to illustrate and mark progress in each area of ministry within the church.
- Determined to caution and counsel ministry leaders, I began writing articles about some of the extreme challenges I faced in the pastorate— including embezzlement, church conflict and constitutional revisions. These were published in *Leadership Journal*[4] and *Christianity Today*[5] books and periodicals.
- Determined to address conflict and dysfunction and to facilitate healing in the church, I established my own non-profit organization, ChurchHealth.
- Determined to help churches recognize the value of older people and offer guidelines for developing powerful and effective ministries, Leona and I wrote and self-published *Amazing Grays: Unleashing the Power of Age in Your Congregation*.[6]
- Determined to challenge the prevalent attitude about retirement, Leona and I produced a short film, *Musical Chairs*.[7]

- Determined to breathe new perspective into how Christian Boomers view and live their second half of life, Leona and I are writing this book, *Third Calling*.

I am wired to look at the world through creative lenses. I've also developed a rather fearless attitude toward fulfilling my creative bent. In my Third Calling, creativity is the fuel that propels me toward innovative ideas and new experiences.

DISCOVERING AND CULTIVATING MY CREATIVE SIDE—Leona

Women are naturally creative, right? At least it seems that my peers excel in sewing, knitting, decorating and painting. I have one friend that makes beautiful little sundresses for her granddaughters—along with matching dresses for their American Girl dolls, accompanying handbags, backpacks, sleeping bags and tents. Another friend paints exquisite watercolors and yet another creates gourmet dinners that could be featured in *Sunset* magazine. Comparatively speaking, I feel like a slug.

However, in studying creativity, I realize I need to be more creative about my definition. In reality, I'm learning to be more resourceful in my approach to problem solving, life planning and personal expression. And, like Richard shared in his story, my life is dotted with, arguably, bursts of brilliance.

Today most of my creativity is expressed through words. I'm learning to write with flair and color. I enjoy playing with graphic arts and developing brochures and newsletters. Our website provides endless opportunities for originality.

Beyond these tangible expressions, my greatest advances in cultivating creativity are in developing new ways of looking at problems, opportunities and challenges. Stepping outside the box, observing issues in new ways—subverting dominant paradigms— takes creativity. Growing and expanding my mature mind energizes my potential to think, act and communicate more creatively.

HOW TO CULTIVATE CREATIVITY—Richard and Leona

Here are some ways to help you think outside the box and begin nurturing and cultivating your creativity:

- Recognize that you are, indeed, creative. When man and woman were brought into being, they were made in God's image—a reflection of the Creator. As sons and daughters of Adam and Eve, we too are filled to the brim with creativity.
- Begin creating something. Pick up a paintbrush, write a poem, try a new recipe, sit down at the piano and plunk out a new tune, or take a walk somewhere you've never been. Expand your mind and allow creativity to grow.
- Try looking at something from a different point of view. Read an editorial and write a rebuttal, listen to a talk show on NPR or visit a church of a different denomination.
- Write an essay or article about a life experience— funny, sad, embarrassing, adventurous—it doesn't matter, just begin putting it into words.
- Take an art, creative writing or gardening class at the local college or university.
- Go on a walk and snap photographs of interesting new things you see. Capture scenes in new lights and different angles. Try zooming and bursting.
- Find ways to stimulate all of your senses. Visit a spice shop and sniff an unfamiliar fragrance. Taste a new food. Tour a textile shop, touch the fabrics and envision the exotic garments you could tailor. Listen to a symphony and visualize playing an original composition. Jump into the worlds of sight, sound, taste, texture and aroma.

- Travel to somewhere you've never been. (See Chapter 12, "Exploring New Worlds.")
- Play a new sport. Expand your understanding of activity, fitness and fun.
- Hike a trail through nature. God's creation will inspire your own creativity—without fail.
- Read a Shakespeare play out loud.
- Try on clothes that are nothing like what you typically wear. Experiment with colors and styles and even prices. You don't have to buy them, just be creative.

CREATIVITY AND OUR AGING JOURNEY
—Richard and Leona

There is no time in life where creativity is more critical than in the season of our Third Calling. Culture constantly tells us how to grow old, how we should think, live and even "retire." Try a "whack on the side of the head" approach to think differently about many areas of life.

For example, your Third Calling may provide an opportunity for you to get very creative about where to live. Think of the possibilities: Perhaps you'll live in a home that you own free and clear. Maybe you will rent an apartment or a beach cabin, or build a tiny house on a plot of land. You could hit the road in an RV, live in a retirement community, or move in with your kids. Possibly you could move to another country, housesit for snowbirds or be a dorm parent in an international school.

Your Third Calling may require you to consider new ways to engage with your family. Adult children and their kids may live in other cities or countries. You may need to move around and live near one family at a time or schedule more visits, or plan interesting reunions. Shake up your family engagements by inviting in-laws to your side-of-the-family events. Commemorate half-birthdays, or consider celebrating Christmas in July. Stay current with technology so you can FaceTime, Skype, Voxer, or Google video your family—wherever they (or you) are.

Your Third Calling may require you to find employment. Try applying for jobs that interest, intrigue and stretch you. Find creative options to transfer your years of experience and knowledge into new expressions and opportunities.

Be creative about ways to stay healthy and fit. Try participating in an exercise group at the gym, community center, or college. Change your diet. Look at wellness from creative, try-anything-once eyes.

Living longer may put a significant strain on your piggy bank if you have one. You may need to sell home and possessions, look for a job, move to a less expensive part of the country, or make a risky investment. It is unlikely that all Boomers will have a predictable income, pension, or even Social Security payments like the generation that preceded us. Creatively managing money, assets and investments is critical and wise.

Creatively planning your day and schedule could be a challenge. It's easy to become bored, or conversely, overcommitted. Learn how to prioritize obligations and commitments. Balance your time to include a variety of activities including service, recreation, solitude, friends, leisure and times for reflection.

Enjoy hobbies and leisure in new, creative ways. Learn new things. Invest time in your interests. Do something you did not have time to do when you were younger.

Aging is the best opportunity of your entire life to nurture your creativity. In fact, graceful and meaningful aging is the outcome of a creative, look-at-it-in-a-new-way mindset. Left unattended, aging can become boring, self-centered and routine.

With a renewed sense of creativity, you can unleash a new life and perspective.

And, if all else fails, you might start with whittling and go from there.

Consider: What challenging area of your life needs a creative perspective or a "whack on the side of the head?"

CHAPTER 10
UNLEASHING YOUR INNER ENTREPRENEUR
By Richard

"Do not follow where the path may lead.
Go instead where there is no path and leave a trail."
—Ralph Waldo Emerson

"Therefore, I remind you to keep ablaze the gift of God that is in
you."
—II Timothy 1:6 HCSB

A NEW BEGINNING

ON MARCH 9, 1995, I DROVE to the office of the Secretary of State in Olympia, Washington and gave birth to a dream. I was there to officially establish my own non-profit organization to fulfill my vision for ministry. My dream was deferred for nine years while I served with two separate ministry organizations. Finally, I mustered the faith and will to start my own organization.

I registered the name, ChurchHealth, to capture my core value that the health of a church is vital to its growth. The ministry organizations I had served with were relatively dysfunctional and I was determined that mine would be different. As I watched leaders in each of these organizations, I recognized, "I can do this and perhaps do it better." On that spring day in my home state's capitol city, I unleashed my inner entrepreneur!

ENTREPRENEUR OF LIFE

Os Guinness, in his book, *Rising to the Call*, states, "As we human beings rise to the call of our Creator, we become sub-creators, entering into our own creativity, artistry and entrepreneurship as made in his image—thus adding to the rich fruitfulness of the universe. Answering the call of our Creator is the ultimate "why" for living, the highest source of purpose in human existence, because it literally transforms us into 'entrepreneurs of life.' "[1]

"The entrepreneur," Guinness adds, "is the person who assumes the responsibility for the creative task, not as an assigned role, a routine function, or an inherited duty, but as a venture of faith, including risk and danger, in order to bring into the world something new and profitable to mankind."[2]

MY FIRST CALLING

My early experience was not as profound as what Guinness suggests, but it did unleash my inner entrepreneur. I became a ventriloquist. As a high school student, I wanted a creative way to express my view of the world, share humor and make money. I had fun building a business with my first dummy, Danny Markham. I still have the first dollar I earned on January 14, 1969 performing at the Phoenix Manor Apartments. Beyond that, I learned insights that have significantly impacted my life and influenced my Third Calling.

There are three roles within ventriloquy. The first, obviously, is the dummy and the second is the ventriloquist. But the third, and the role that goes unseen is the scriptwriter, the composer of a sketch, or schtick (a comic theme or gimmick). While the ventriloquist manipulates the movements of the dummy, it is the scriptwriter that controls what is said. The ventriloquist and the scriptwriter may be the same, but never the ventriloquist and the dummy.

Later, as an adult sitting in my office early in my career I understood my supervisors expected me to follow the script and promote their materials. It was clear, "I am just the dummy in this organization." It was in that moment my consciousness awakened to the realities of the world around me. I call it my *epiphany*. I could choose to be the dummy, the ventriloquist, or the scriptwriter. I began seeing this same theme played out in other areas. Authors are scriptwriters. Movies are based on their books, requiring a screenplay and script before a film can be produced. Actors then portray the characters represented in the screenplay that was based on the book. Say what you may, that was my paradigm shifting epiphany that unleashed my inner entrepreneur. That day it became overwhelmingly clear: I wanted to be the scriptwriter, not the dummy.

MY SECOND CALLING

It took serving in another organization for six years before I was able to write my own script. I determined I would start my organization. I bought the book, *How to Start a Non-Profit Organization*,[3] and began reading it, highlighting and flagging relevant pages. I talked to people who had launched their own organizations and gleaned from them what I could. I met with an accountant, a former IRS employee, to gain insight into how to position the organization to become a tax-exempt, 501(c)(3) organization. I consulted a lawyer on how to write Articles of Incorporation and secured a template from him. I discovered the six elements required to launch a non-profit organization:

1. An incorporator.
2. A name (reserved in advance with the Secretary of State).
3. A governing board consisting of three founding members.

4. A designated registered agent (somebody for the state to send mail to).

5. An EIN (employee identification number secured through the federal government).

6. Lastly, $40 for the Washington incorporation fee.

Instead of simply mailing the application to the Secretary of State in Olympia, Washington, I chose to complete the process in person. I set aside the entire day for the task (this is a government agency). But after an unexpectedly brief wait in line, it was my turn. I handed the completed Articles of Incorporation to the clerk, expecting she would tell me to come back after lunch for my approval. Instead, she said, "Wait here." In less than ten minutes she came back with my approved Articles of Incorporation stamped:

FILED:

STATE OF WASHINGTON, MAR 9 1995

RALPH MUNRO SECRETARY OF STATE

I paid the $40 incorporation fee. I received the UBI number and the Certification of Incorporation for ChurchHealth. With that, I was out the door.

It took me nine long years from my first inclination of starting my own organization to get to this point. Finally "ChurchHealth" became a bona fide legal entity. The next steps required securing a Master Business License from the State, holding an initial board meeting to formally elect officers and authorizing the opening of a bank account in the organization's name. I wasn't done yet. I wanted to obtain IRS recognition as a 501(c)(3) organization, which would allow us to accept donations and apply for grants. Read Sandra Deja's book, *Prepare Your Own 501(c)(3) Application*[4] to learn more about this process. I wish I had met her years earlier as I started going down this path.

We celebrated ChurchHealth's 20th Anniversary in 2015. During this time, I have helped at least a dozen individuals discover their inner entrepreneur by coaching them in the process of incorporating a non-profit and applying for 501(c)(3) status. I taught a class in social entrepreneurship at a local university for students interested in making a difference in the world. Recently, Leona and I had the opportunity to travel to India to lead a class on entrepreneurship for college students.

The point is: You too can unleash your inner entrepreneur and establish a business, ministry or non-profit service organization.

UNLEASHING YOUR INNER ENTREPRENEUR

While my experience is in the non-profit sector, the same principles apply to anyone interested in starting a business or a for-profit corporation. Here is a summary of what I believe it takes to Unleash Your Inner Entrepreneur.

- Believe that you can do it. You don't need anyone's permission to start a business or to launch a corporation, be it for profit or non-profit. You're no DUMMY!
- Realize you have something to offer the world. It might be a skill, a product or experience in a certain field. Take the time to discover what that might be. My friend Dan, a marketing consultant, recently told me about a random encounter with a restaurant worker who had an idea for a better way to floss teeth. Dan helped him get his product to market and it is now finding its way into major retail outlets.
- Seek help. Find mentors who can help you achieve your goals. I joined Christian Leadership Alliance and attended their national conferences to find the resources I needed at the time. I spoke with others who had gone through the same processes and

gleaned information from them.

- Research the legal components of starting a business or a corporation. Determine if you need a CPA or an attorney for specific aspects of your endeavor.
- Count the cost of time and effort that it will take you to become an entrepreneur. Once you give birth to your idea, you still have to raise this child you've created. Many visionaries are not typically wired to deal with the administrative details of a business or a non-profit organization. Decide if you really need your own business or organization, or could you partner with an existing entity and avoid the hassle?
- Recognize you may not be in a position to make a complete leap into the uncertain world of the entrepreneur at this time. Instead begin small with something on the side. Start a home based business. Begin to write a blog or even a book that can give voice to your ideas. Begin to strategize a trajectory that creates a new path for your future alongside your job or career.
- Believe you have something to say to the world. Fifteen years ago, Leona and I felt we had a message to share. We learned how to write, edit, layout and self-publish our book *Amazing Grays: Unleashing the Power of Age in Your Congregation*.[5] We enlisted the talent of family members to design the cover, proofread the book and format the pages. We contracted with a local graphics company to print 1,650 copies. The book became the basis for seminars we began conducting

regionally and then nationally. It led to a contract with our denomination to lead the older adult ministry initiative, which we did for a decade. Now, once again, we have a message and are addressing the world through this book, *Third Calling*. Believe you have something to say, unleash your inner entrepreneur and find a way to get your message out there.

MY THIRD CALLING

Recently I realized I wanted to put all of my energies into our non-profit organization, so I transitioned out of my full-time job as an Executive Pastor at a megachurch. Leona and I began developing what has now become the heart of our next phase of life, work and ministry: Re-Ignite. This initiative focuses on helping leading edge boomers re-discover their life's purpose and calling for this next stage of life. We developed a business plan, wrote curriculum, produced a workshop/retreat format and hired a website developer. We offered the Re-Ignite curriculum to our own church first and then expanded to other congregations and retreat centers. We received invitations to travel as far as Sweden, New Zealand, Australia and India. As the opportunities increased, we realized it was time to pursue our larger goals in life full-time. It was time once again to unleash our inner entrepreneur. This book, *Third Calling*, is only the beginning.

In the movie, *Stranger than Fiction*, IRS auditor Harold Crick (Will Ferrell) sits in a coffee shop owned by Ana, an anti-establishment baker (Maggie Gyllenhaal). She refuses to pay taxes on munitions, which is why Harold is there. During their conversation, while she is tempting him with her latest concoctions, he asks her where she learned to bake. When she replies, "In college," he mistakenly assumes it was a cooking school, when in fact she attended Harvard Law School. But her passion for baking overcame her discipline for the study of law. She explains, "At the end of the semester, I had twenty-seven study partners, eight Mead journals filled with recipes and a D average. So I dropped out. I just figured if I was going to make the world a better place I would do it with cookies."[6]

This example brings our discussion about unleashing your inner entrepreneur right down to where we can all relate—like the joy of baking delicious cookies. Unleashing our inner entrepreneur is about figuring out who we are, why we are here and following our passion for offering something of value in the world.

Unleashing my inner entrepreneur required me becoming aware of my own possibilities and potential. Many inner voices were telling me I had to work for someone else or be hired by somewhere else. It wasn't until I had my epiphany that I realized I had it within me.

It seems everything I needed to learn about unleashing my inner entrepreneur I learned from my dummies!

CALLING ALL GIRLS—Leona

As a young teenager, I eagerly awaited that time of the month when the magazine, *Calling All Girls*,[7] came to my mailbox. It was chock full of things I needed to know, like how to grow long nails, have shiny hair and tips for throwing a great party. There was something else included in my subscription: the right to be a part of an exclusive group of pubescent girls who lived all across the nation. I belonged to a subculture—Boomer females and we were the center point of an entire movement called *feminism*.

The very word made the hair stand up on my pastor's neck— and probably on the neck of every male in my orbit. It meant that women were finding a voice, a purpose and even a cause. I didn't burn my bra, but I did
long to understand what my potential might be if I were considered equal to my male friends.

Now, decades later, I still belong in a cohort of Boomer babes. Some of us have accomplished great things including professional careers, motherhood and marriage. We've watched our young leave the nest (and sometimes return) and we've said long goodbyes to parents. We are at a new stage of life where we are yearning for meaning, significance—and a Third Calling.

Interestingly, we are also dominating our generation, in numbers at least. Statistics say nearly 15% of the U.S. population, are women over age 65. Sadly, older women also fill the ranks of those living in poverty. Studies show that as many as 60% of women over age 65 (living alone or with a spouse) have incomes insufficient to cover basic, daily expenses.[8] Many are not ready, financially, socially or emotionally, to thrive in this season of life.

So, I'm "calling all girls" to once again find a voice, a purpose and even a cause for which to live in this unique season. Married or single, the possibilities for women to impact the world are great.

Consider some of my friends who have created enterprises, accomplished amazing feats, or re-invented themselves for this season. Gwen, in her mid-70s applied her expertise in education and became the president of a struggling university; Norma, widowed in her mid-50s, went on to pursue a career in politics and now serves as a congresswoman in our state; Susie created her own drama business and now travels around the country performing monologues about women of faith; Elisa, having struggled with health issues for years, began consulting others about wellness and developed a thriving vitamin and supplement business. The stories go on and on.

The question is, can we, as women who are "coming of age," seize the day and follow our Third Calling? Can we take our life experience and give birth to new enterprises and endeavors?

Clearly, the principles of the Third Calling are for both

men and women. At the same, time, one brutal fact we face is that a woman's life expectancy in the U.S. has climbed to over 80, whereas men's is late 70s. If we find ourselves dwelling in retirement communities where two-thirds of the residents are women, can we forego the cultural expectations to simply sit and knit and live on substandard government assistance? Or will we use our experience and talents to forge new pathways, develop new products and services—and unleash our feminine inner entrepreneur?

Amy Gossman coaches midlife entrepreneurs wanting to launch new businesses and services. In an article she wrote for the National Association of Baby Boomer Women,[9] she identifies seven traits boomer women entrepreneurs have in common.

1. Autonomy—they want to call their own shots.
2. Resilience—they bounce back from setbacks; they've weathered life's ups and downs.
3. Initiative—they are self-starters.
4. Confidence—they believe in themselves and get others to believe in them too.
5. Intuitive—they analyze problems, but they also trust their intuition.
6. Decisive—they have had a lifetime of experience to fine-tune their decision making ability.
7. Connects—they have well-developed networks and re-lationships.

Does this describe you? It may be time to unleash your feminine inner entrepreneur.

Some time ago, Richard was a candidate for the position of senior pastor at a church in Colorado. I was invited to join him in an interview with the deacon board. After several hours of interrogation, the attention turned to me and the predictable question was asked. "So, if your husband is the pastor here, what will you do?" I knew they wanted to hear that I would staff the nursery, play the piano and meet with the ladies. Instead, I answered, "Well, if he gets sick, I preach." Being a church unaccustomed to women speaking from the pulpit, the response was stunned silence. Of course, we all laughed, Richard eventually accepted the job and I developed my piano playing skills and drank a lot of tea. However, my feeble attempt to define my abilities became the starting point for unleashing my inner entrepreneur. I began writing, speaking, studying and eventually, found my second calling in leadership and management.

Today, I'm living my Third Calling. I'm still an entrepreneur, writing, speaking and developing products and services for Boomers.

I've found my voice and you're hearing it.

> *"A woman is like a tea bag – you never know*
> *how strong she is until she gets into hot water."*
> – Eleanor Roosevelt

Exercise—type 20 times:

Now is the time for all good women to come to the aid of their country.

Consider: Given the opportunity, what kind of business, non-profit organization or service would you launch?

CHAPTER 11

HEARING THE ONE WHO CALLS
By Leona

"In the silence of the heart, God speaks.
If you face God in prayer and silence, God will speak to you."
—Mother Teresa

God called to him out of the bush, "Moses, Moses!"
And he said, "Here I am."
—Exodus 3:4 ESV

I HAD TO CHECK THE boxes every night and I couldn't fall asleep until I did. As a teenager, I kept a diary and on every day's entry, I listed three activities. Each had a box next to it, so as I completed the task, I could check it off: (1) brush my hair 100 strokes, (2) Do 100 sit-ups and (3) Have my devotions.

Call me compulsive or dedicated—both would be accurate. I was compelled to do whatever necessary to have shiny hair and a healthy body. And, I knew to be a good Christian, I had to have a quiet time with God—or as my youth leaders called it, my QT.

Now, in my seventh decade of life, I've learned that such rigidity verges on legalism. Today my hair is shiny because of the expensive shampoo I use. I gave up on sit-ups and am happy to exercise just enough to be healthy. I'm viewing life with a new set of eyes these days and that includes how I seek God. A checklist may assure that I've completed the task, but it doesn't guarantee that I've experienced the Holy.

I am not alone in yearning for a meaningful connection with

God that goes beyond the fill-in-the-blank devotions or quick downloadable inspirations. Boomers, whether they've grown up in the church or have followed Christ later in life, seem to have a deep longing for the Sacred. I see it in the eyes of fellow participants in the spirituality and aging gatherings I attend. Frankly, I see it in the eyes of people sitting by me in the pew.

I understand the importance of disciplines—Bible Study, prayer and worshipping with a community of believers. These practices prop up my Christian life, support my wobbly soul and teach me the truths of my faith. But after experiencing losses, traumas and disappointments, as well as joys and triumphs, I realize God is in new places, fresh experiences and raw encounters.

As I seek to live my Third Calling, I hunger to know the One who has called me. I long to go beyond briefly touching the pages of Scripture and go deeper to understand the story behind the story. Dr. William Thomas,[1] noted geriatric physician and author, believes the older we get, the more we can understand the multiple layers of the what is happening around us. We see life in 3-D, or, what he calls, "getting the gist." As we age, he says, we observe life with profound new insights that the young are hard pressed to match.

Getting the gist of God's story demands more than spending a few minutes reading a devotional and checking a box. As I pursue knowing God and "enjoying and glorifying him forever,"[2] I am obliged to open my heart and mind to more thoughtful study, new experiences, new pathways of worship and new avenues of encountering the Holy. As I strive to understand and follow my Third Calling, I am stirred to know more deeply the One who calls me.

Gary Thomas, in his classic book, *Sacred Pathways*, suggests that each of us may encounter God in unique ways, according to our spiritual temperaments. Some see Him in nature and creation. Others encounter Him intensely through simple, quiet contemplation and meditation; others through sacred liturgy and ritual and still others through active service.[3]

The notion that I can encounter the King of Kings through his Word and worship Him in multiple settings helps me get the gist of God's greater story in my life and the world. Today I will stand on the shore and marvel at the power of the ocean waves and experience the supremacy of the Creator. Tomorrow, I may kneel in the sanctuary of a grand cathedral and worship His Majesty, the Sovereign God. On Saturday morning, alone in my living room, I can play the piano, sing the traditional hymns of my faith and feel the familiarity of the Lord's presence. One day, in serving soup to a homeless mom and her kids, I will deeply sense the profound compassion and love of the Great Shepherd. Experiencing God in these ways moves me beyond the pages of my daily devotions.

HEARING THE ONE WHO CALLS

Two thousand years ago, Jesus said, "Follow me" to twelve men who were as unique as any humans you'll ever find. Each of them had very different life experiences from the other. Each was established in his career. Some had families and responsibilities in their communities and synagogues. When Jesus called them, they recognized the power that compelled them to follow. Committing their lives to Jesus radically transformed their lives and occupations. Being one of Jesus' disciples was their Second Calling; changing the world was their Third Calling.

Moses was settled into a routine out on the backside of the desert. He had family responsibilities and livestock to manage. And then the day came when God called—rather dramatically through a burning bush. Moses recognized power that compelled him to follow. His First Calling included being educated and groomed for leadership in the courts of Pharaoh; his Second Calling lived out on the desert was not nearly as glamorous as the First. Now, God was calling him to change the course of history. Leading the people of Israel out of captivity and into the Promised Land was an exotic Third Calling.

The point is, Moses heard the One who calls—and he listened.

Think of the men and women whose stories are recorded in Scripture, those who heard the One who calls. In responding, they found purpose and passion in life—and a Third Calling. Consider Esther, Noah, Jonah, David, Paul, Lydia and Timothy, to name a few. Had they not listened and responded, they would have missed seeing God do "exceedingly more than they could think or imagine." (Eph. 3:20) They would have missed the purpose of their Third Calling.

Throughout this book, we are challenging you to consider what God is calling you to be and do in this season of life. We are sharing our journey as well as the stories of others. We are showing you the Re-Ignite process as a way to help you discover and understand your unique design, values, gifts, passions and purpose. When all is said and done, the assessments and the introspection are only tools to help you recognize what God is doing in you at this stage of life. To understand God's purpose for our lives, we simply must listen to His voice.

What is God saying to you? How do you hear the One who is calling?

1. The place to begin is in the Bible.
   What scriptures speak to your heart and how do you hear the Lord's voice as you read them?
   If you don't know where to start, consider reading these accounts of men and women:
   Abraham—Genesis 12
   Moses—Exodus 3
   Elijah—I Kings 19
   Esther—Esther 1-5
   Jesus' disciples—Matthew 4; Mark 1
   Paul—Acts 9
   Peter—John 1:42; Acts 5
2. Looking back over the journey of your life, how has the Lord built a theme into the circumstances?

Where have you heard His voice or sensed His touch during those times?

3. Pour your heart out to God, then be still and listen. Take the time to seek him and worship him—in nature, in a cathedral, in the quiet of your home. To put it simply: pray.

TURN YOUR EYES UPON JESUS

As I write this, the old hymn, *Turn Your Eyes Upon Jesus*, is playing on my Pandora playlist. As a teenager, I tried so hard to find God and know what he wanted me to be and do. I now recall the words to this song, which we sang at the end of every Youth for Christ rally. Today, as it did then, the words remind me to stop, be quiet and listen to the One who calls me. The One who will tell me what he wants me to do and be.

> *Turn your eyes upon Jesus*
> *Look full in His wonderful face*
> *And the things of Earth will grow strangely dim*
> *In the light of His glory and grace.*[4]
> —Helen Lemmel, 1922, Public Domain

Turn your eyes to the One who created you. Turn your ears to hear the One who calls you.

He has a plan and a purpose for you.

It's your Third Calling.

You were meant for this!

Consider: Write a prayer to the One who is calling you. Share your heart, your fears, your questions. Spend some time in silence. Listen.

PART THREE

EMBRACE THE JOURNEY

CHAPTER 12
EXPLORING NEW WORLDS
by Richard

"The more that you read, the more things you will know.
The more you learn, the more places you'll go!"
—Dr. Seuess

"The LORD had said to Abram, 'Leave your country, your people
and your father's household and go to the land I will show you.'"
—Genesis 12:1

RICK STEVES DEVELOPED A BUSINESS out of his passion for travel. His international headquarters sit in an unassuming building in downtown Edmonds, Washington. When it came time for me to take a sabbatical a few years ago, we tapped into all the resources his company had to offer. The business that began as *Europe Through The Back Door*, is now recognized as *Rick Steves*.[1] We studied his books about the countries we intended to visit, spoke with his travel consultants and bought our Eurail passes at his offices. Our goal was to visit ten countries in six weeks. On next to the last day in Europe we had only visited nine, so we took a one-day trip from Tallin, Estonia to Helsinki, Finland to complete our journey.

The strength of Rick Steves' approach is that he and his tour guides have traveled to every place found in their guidebooks. His books and videos provide you detailed instructions on transportation, the best places to stay near transportation hubs and recommended local cuisine. The instructions are specific enough to tell you which direction to turn when you get off the train and how many feet or meters to the nearest recommended lodging. We relied on his instructions and followed them precisely. It gave us the confidence to venture out on our own in countries where the language, culture and currency were all foreign to us.

Travel opportunities in our Third Calling season have stretched us beyond anything we could have imagined. Our first big travel adventure was to Kauai, Hawaii. Some friends of ours heard we had never been to Hawaii and said "that's just not right." They gave us the use of a timeshare for three weeks and $1,000 spending money. We had award miles to cover airfare, so off we went. Without a doubt, the experience was the most adventurous, relaxing and romantic escapade of our lives to that point. We learned about Hawaiian culture, swam with the sea turtles and drenched ourselves in sunshine. Hawaii opened our hearts and minds to the possibilities of travel. In the past decade we have explored many new worlds and some of our encounters have deeply influenced the direction of our Third Calling.

While on a sabbatical in 2013 we set a goal of visiting 10 countries in six weeks:

- On the cliffs overlooking the beaches of Normandy, we pictured what thousands of troops faced as they landed on the beaches of France and attempted to storm the cliffs against the barrage of German guns concealed behind the concrete bunkers.
- In the American cemetery, we walked amidst the thousands of gravesites marking the soldiers who had sacrificed everything to defeat an evil tyranny.
- In Dachau, we toured the gas chambers and the crematoriums used to exterminate Jews during WWII.
- In Berlin, we observed a country facing its dark

past while forging a new future. We walked freely from the East to the West, which would have been a death walk in the 60s, 70s and 80s when the Berlin wall was still standing.

- In Salzburg, Austria we went on the "Sound of Music" tour and kissed in front of the famous gazebo where Liesl and Rolf danced.
- In Gimmewald, Switzerland we rode the cable car to the top of the Swiss Alps and viewed the world from a whole new perspective.

Our most meaningful opportunities to explore new worlds were in connection with short-term mission trips we took with teams of older adults. Traveling with a purpose greatly expands your horizons and may shape your Third Calling:

- In Estonia, we visited churches that were re-opened after 40 years of Soviet rule. We stood on the Song Festival grounds where Estonians participated in the singing revolution that brought about their freedom in 1989 without a shot fired. We stayed in a friend's apartment, which had been returned to them after the collapse of the Soviet Union.
- In Riga, Latvia we worshiped in a church that remained open during the entire Soviet era thanks to the boldness of the pastor who defied the KGB.
- In Nicaragua, we met families who lived in abject poverty but exhibited joy and happiness despite their conditions in life. We saw people living in the dump outside of Managua sorting through garbage for something of value.
- In Moldova, we met elderly people whose entire life savings had evaporated when the Soviet Union collapsed. We stayed in the home of a pastor—an

apartment in a concrete Soviet-era high-rise apartment.

- In Belize we walked the alleys of a village and observed the impact rampant drug use had on its children and families.

- In India, we saw both the poorest of the poor as well as extreme opulence. We met students who came from the lowest class of Indian society, who were now being given a chance to pursue higher education.

- In Sweden, we facilitated Re-Ignite events for leaders two years in a row. We also visited my third cousin and her family in the northernmost part of Sweden from where my great-grandfather emigrated while my cousin's great-grandfather remained in Sweden. We enjoyed a reunion with 36 of my most distant relatives in the land of my origins. We visited Leona's family near Linköping and stood on the land her great-grandfather farmed before taking his family to the U.S.

In each place visited, we confronted new and strange customs, cuisines, culture and currencies. We no sooner crossed a border when our money from the former country became invalid. The people spoke a different language than those in the last country. We had to learn to adapt to entirely new environments.

We have more places we want to visit. As Susan Sontag said, "I haven't been everywhere, but it's on my list."

Exploring new worlds opens your mind to new possibilities in your Third Calling. Traveling in a foreign country and culture where you do not speak the language or know how to calculate the currency, takes you out of your comfort zone. It makes you dependent on others. It stretches you. You learn you are not in control. You ask a lot of questions, like "Do you speak English?" Fortunately in most of the well-traveled European countries, you can find someone who speaks English enough to get you to the train station.

St. Augustine said, "The world is a book and those who do not travel read only one page."

Of course, travel is not the only way to explore new worlds. There are many other avenues to expand your horizons.

- Participate in Lifelong Learning. There are many opportunities to take classes in local colleges and universities, as well as online classes. In Sun City, Arizona the Lifelong Learning Club offers about 40 lectures and multi-sessions each semester at the Fairway Recreation Center.[2] Topics include art, music, history, health and well-being, finances, current affairs and entertainment.

- Become a "Road Scholar."[3] The original "Elderhostel" exists to inspire adults to learn, discover and travel. It offers 5,500 educational tours in all 50 states and 150 countries.

- Volunteer in an area that you have never served before. Recently we enjoyed an evening in a pastor's home in Sun City Grand, Arizona and had an opportunity to ask, "Does everyone just come down here to play?" He informed us that many do, but after the initial exhilaration of being able to indulge in a life of leisure, many begin to seek more meaningful involvements. Sun City has one of the highest per capita number of volunteers of any city in the country. An administrator in the Dysart School District, told us the same. His district has scores of retired volunteers in their schools. He doesn't know where they would be without them.

- Visit a homeless shelter. My sister and her husband live in an area of Seattle that has recently become an enclave of homeless people camping out in their RVs overnight. Drug deals are ongoing and trash is piling up. The mayor has declared a state of emergency regarding the homeless crisis. Some of their neighbors are militant about ridding the neighborhood of the homeless while others realize their plight makes them vulnerable. My sister has taken on the challenge of advocating for a solution rather than only wanting to rid the neighborhood of the problem. A visit to a homeless shelter or a tent city might provide you with a greater understanding of the plight of others.

- Attend conferences that challenge your presuppositions and expand your thinking. For example, Seattle University hosts a conference each year entitled "The Search for Meaning Book Festival."[4] It features authors from a variety of backgrounds and viewpoints. And while I don't share the same worldview as all of them, I can glean insights from the keynote speakers and sessions offered. The National Council on Aging (NCOA)[5] and the American Society on Aging (ASA)[6] have combined to host one annual national conference. The Religion and Spirituality Forum is broad enough to encompass a wide range of religious and spiritual worldviews.

- Watch a PBS program about a particular country. Before traveling to India, last year we devoured everything we could in order to learn about the country where our son and family are living for two years. PBS had a six program series entitled, "*The Story of India*."[7] Programs are offered daily featuring distant lands, cultures and experiences.

- Watch a Rick Steves travel program to learn how to visit and experience another part of the world.

- Reach out and meet new people. For many, this can be a

challenge. It takes energy to initiate a conversation and ask questions. During the month of writing this book, we found many new opportunities to meet people from all around the country. And in a retirement haven like Arizona, everyone seems willing to talk. Leading with a question about the weather or the part of the country people come from is an easy way to start the conversation.

In the movie, *UP*,[8] the young Carl Frederickson meets his future bride, Ellie, when they are children playing in an abandoned house. She created a scrapbook and named it *My Adventure Book*. It contained a vision of traveling to South America and visiting Paradise Falls. Her enthusiastic proclamation to young Carl was, "Adventure is out there!" Then throughout her adult life, she documents the adventures that she and Carl had over their years, in spite of having to spend their vacation savings on unexpected life events. When she takes ill in her latter years, she passes off the adventure book to him. Unbeknownst to him, the adventure book is not about their vacation dreams to visit Paradise Falls, but rather a documentary of their life together. You don't have to travel the world to have great adventures. Adventure is out there wherever we are and in whatever we are doing.

Exploring new worlds, be they real or virtual, can be an exciting part of life in your Third Calling. You may find a whole new dimension to life you never before encountered.

Consider: Imagine having a cup of tea in a place you've never been before.
Where would it be? Who would you share tea with?
What are the sounds and sites you imagine seeing?
What would you like to know about this place?

CHAPTER 13
TAKING THE LEAP
By Richard

*"You cannot discover new oceans
unless you have the courage to lose sight of the shore."*
—Unknown

"With man this is impossible, but with God all things are possible."
—Matthew 19:26

"FOLLOW ME," I YELLED TO my entourage as I leaped over a bush to demonstrate my athletic prowess.

Failing to notice there was a significant trench on the other side, I did not land on my feet, but rather on my back with a thud! I forgot that age-old axiom, "Look before you leap." Since I disappeared from their sight, no one else took me up on my challenge.

2016 is a leap year in our calendar. The idea of a "leap" year is familiar to me—I've taken a few.

In January 1965, my parents took a trip from Montana to the Southwest to explore job opportunities for my father and educational opportunities for our family. He walked into Barrows Furniture on Scottsdale Road in Phoenix to apply for a job. He was hired on the spot to manage the carpet department. Three weeks later, we sold our family home in Kalispell, Montana and headed down Highway 93 to Phoenix.

Leaping, I have discovered, is a part of my DNA.

Since that first life-altering leap in 1965, I have taken many other leaps. One was my decision to leave my first pastorate before securing my next placement. Leona and I drove to Deception Pass in Washington State, where a dramatic bridge connects the mainland to Whidbey Island. I felt as if I had jumped off the bridge career-wise and was in free fall. But within a matter of weeks, we had received a call to our next assignment in Colorado.

We leaped again from our pastorate in Colorado to join an organization in Southern California. After just a year with them, however, we made the leap back to the Pacific Northwest, with no jobs, only a partial support base. Within 30 days, Leona had secured a job at the hospital and I was offered an interim role in a local church. Following six years serving with yet another organization, we leaped again to form our own non-profit organization.

When finances were getting tight in 2004, we leaped again to return to Seattle where Leona took a job as a program director in a senior adult community. I was invited to join the staff of a large church, where I eventually became the Executive Pastor. I stayed in that church for ten years. But as I approached my 65th birthday, I concluded it was time to leap again, this time back to work at our non-profit organization that we had started twenty years earlier. We had been developing our Re-Ignite initiative for several years and it became apparent that if we were going to follow God's call, achieve our potential with it and realize our goals, we would both need to be giving our full attention to the effort.

WHAT I'VE LEARNED ABOUT LEAPING

- Leaping is scary business. While traveling in New Zealand, we rode the elevator to the top of the Sky Tower in Auckland. We watched as people paid to leap off the 1,076-foot building to the ground below. Yes, they were tightly hooked to guide wires all the way down, but it was nevertheless a frightening thing to watch. We passed on the opportunity. Leaping from one job to another, or from a tall building can elicit a lot of fear. But it is also exhilarating.

- Leaping is sometimes necessary to achieve your life goals. A plaque on my desk reminds me, "A ship in a harbor is safe, but that is not what ships are made for." Unless we are willing to leave the comfort of the port, we will never get to where we were meant to go.
- Leaping can result in new, unforeseen opportunities. Karsten Solheim was in his 50s the first time he went golfing. He didn't like the feel of the clubs and being an engineer, he set about to design a new putter. When his new putter struck the ball it made a "ping" sound and the rest is history. He left his job at GE and launched the PING golf company in Phoenix, Arizona.
- Leaping can also be catastrophic. Sometimes a business may fail or an idea may flop. A move to a new part of the country may not turn out as planned. A new relationship may not work out.

SOME THINGS TO CONSIDER BEFORE YOU LEAP

- Don't leap from your job or career out of frustration or anger. It's hard to recover from leaving a job badly.
- Don't leap without a plan—unless you have to. I still prefer to have a plan of how and where I'm going to land (but I haven't always).
- Consider the impact on others. Your decision to leap has far reaching implications for those closest to you.

Children are affected by a move, as are your friends and colleagues.

- Don't make enemies of your current employer if you are leaping to take another job. You never know when you might need a good reference or even when they might want you back. As a matter of fact, when my successor left, my former pastor called me and invited me to come back and serve for six months as an interim Executive Pastor.

GOING WITHOUT KNOWING

One of my favorite stories in the Old Testament of the Bible is of Abram, who took a leap—going without knowing where he would end up.

"The LORD had said to Abram, 'Leave your country,
your people and your father's household and go to the land I
will show you...' Abram left, as the LORD had told him;
and Lot went with him.
Abram was seventy-five years old when he set out
from Haran.
He took his wife Sarai, his nephew Lot, all the possessions
they had acquired in Haran and they set out for the land of
Canaan and they arrived there."
—Genesis 12:1,4-5

At 75 years of age Abram would have been a likely candidate for retirement by today's standards. But God had a whole new plan for his life and his legacy. He took the leap and followed the call of God upon his life, going without knowing how it would all turn out. He truly found and followed his Third Calling, and a new name, Abraham.

The theme of "going without knowing," has inspired me at times to take a leap, even when I didn't know the end game. In each time, I have experienced the faithfulness of God to provide and to show me the next steps. So maybe there is a time to leap, even when we aren't sure of the outcome.

Weigh the risks, count the cost—and go ahead—take the LEAP!

Consider: What would it take for you to take a risk, a leap—to go without knowing?

CHAPTER 14

NAVIGATING WHITE WATERS
by Leona

"Your life is not going to be easy and it should not be easy.
It ought to be hard. It ought to be radical; it ought to be restless;
it ought to lead you to places you'd rather not go."
—Henry Nouwen

"When you go through deep waters, I will be with you.
When you go through rivers of difficulty, you will not drown."
— Isaiah 43:2 NLT

"YOU'RE NOT GOING DOWN THE chutes like that are you?" Those were the last words we had heard before our inflatable raft plunged over what appeared to be a harmless, flat, smooth rock formation. Puddles of lazy water lapping against a table of stone suddenly turned into raging waters destined to plunge straight down. People on the shore were waving their arms and shouting. Naively, we waved back with thumbs up and high fives. We were soon lost in a haze of white bubbles and cold murk.

It all started so peacefully. We were floating down the river on a lazy afternoon; enjoying the sights, companionship and the common purpose of just getting down the river. Like life, something happened we weren't prepared for.

What resulted was near disaster as we were thrown from the comforts of the raft, we splashed into the cold glacier-fed stream, held our breath and plummeted. Our angels were on red alert that day and we survived.

Some of what we learned from those white waters continues to impact us as we focus on our Third Calling.

WHITE WATER EXPERIENCES

This season of our life is filled with white water experiences. The years between age 60 and 80 may be the most dynamic of the entire life span. Dynamic, meaning we experience the most change, loss and even transformation than any other life season. Living out our Third Calling takes some skill in navigating the white waters as well as the calm ones.

In Chapter 4 we described the *Voyage of Life* paintings on display in the National Gallery of Art in Washington D.C. As we explained, the artist Thomas Cole portrayed adulthood, or what we would call midlife, as dreadfully foreboding. The man in the boat was nearly obscured by the dark, ominous skies, scraggly landscape and the impending doom of rough, white waters. If we now presume there is a painting missing—this new stage we are living in—then we are in the midst of the white waters. We're going down the chutes!

How do we successfully navigate our voyage?

EXPECT THE UNEXPECTED

Don't be surprised by change, pain, or even disaster. Life is filled with difficulties and it should not catch us unaware when suffering enters our life. It may shock, disorient, or even dismay us. But, we should expect it. When tubing down the river, we should have anticipated the terrain might change and our smooth sailing could come to an abrupt end.

Difficulties are a regular part of life. All you have to do is look at your life story to see that pain, disappointment and change may be the only constant. Frank Sinatra understood the ups and downs of life when, in 1966, he recorded the song, *That's Life*:

"I've been up and down and over and out...that's life."[1]

From a Christian perspective, we know that troubles will come our way.

"Beloved, do not be surprised at the fiery trial when
it comes upon you to test you, as though
something strange were happening to you."

—1 Peter 4:12 ESV

We also know there is purpose and redemption in our pain. Scripture reminds us over and over again that, no matter what form the white water takes, God will be with us.

That's life.

BE PRESENT IN THE PAIN

Our friend, Marcia, is confronting stage four breast cancer. In the midst of ministering with abused women around the world, she received the universally dreaded news that the Big C was taking over major parts of her body including breast tissue, bones and the lining of her lungs. Marcia entertains all of the *Why me?*, *What if?* or *Why now?* questions, especially during the long days of chemotherapy and nausea. At the same time, she is doing an amazing thing. Marcia is embracing the experience and paying attention to its lessons about grace, joy and peace. Every day she posts her "Grace Sighting" on Facebook. With a heart filled with gratitude she shares about cards received, visits she enjoyed and funny things her grandsons said. She is present in the pain. It is not enjoyable, but it is not wasted.

Ward is a pastor, author and a good friend of ours. Last year, his wife, the love of his life, died of pancreatic cancer. Her encounter with the disease was indescribably difficult, yet through it all, she and Ward determined to not waste the experience. They wanted to capture the extreme grief and the mystical joy and show others how God's grace truly is sufficient. Ward paid attention to the pain. He recently released the book, *Sacred Journey*,[2] about his and Dixie's story. It gives us a glimpse into the road that leads from pain to heaven.

Whatever the white waters, whatever unexpected occurs, be present. Pay attention.

> *"Many are the afflictions of the righteous,*
> *but the Lord delivers him out of them all."*
>
> —Psalm 34:19 ESV

FIND SUPPORT

Line your riverbanks with those who encourage you, speak truth and pick you up when you go under.

"Two things are ruining the lives of people in our age 55+ community," Jack, our Arizona friend, told us. "Depression and alcoholism. It's hidden and it's lethal."

White water can push one under. While sucking in mud and water and there is no sky in sight, it may seem impossible to hang on. Some turn to substances to numb the sense of doom. An estimated 80,000 of this country's nearly eight million alcoholics are people over age 65. The problem is multiplying as the vast numbers of Boomers age. According to researchers studying and writing for the Society for the Study of Addiction, the number of adults aged 50 or older with substance abuse disorder is projected to double from 2.8 million (annual average) in 2002-06 to 5.7 million in 2020.[3]

To fully live your Third Calling, you have to learn to navigate the white waters in healthy ways. Most people, especially those dealing with depression and alcoholism, need the support of others. Groups such as Celebrate Recovery[4] or Alcoholics Anonymous[5] are essential resources for those struggling with addictions. Counseling and support groups are critical for those debilitated by depression and sadness.

Issues such as these are delicate, complex and difficult to navigate. Our plea is that you don't go it alone. Get help.

PUTTING YOUR LIFE BACK TOGETHER

Slowly and purposefully, work to put the pieces of your life back together. Remember, it will look different after surviving white water.

Going through the chutes was traumatic. Our bodies literally flew through the air, our inflatable disappeared and we fell into a deep and quiet pool beneath the falls. Spitting mud and water from our mouths, we re-emerged and began a frantic effort to make sense of what happened. Frankly, we were happy just to find each other.

Devastating experiences are at the very least, disorienting. Sometimes they completely demolish everything.

Recently, Jane listened as the neurologist reported her husband has dementia. The life they planned hit white water. They have to reassemble the pieces.

John and Carrie lost everything they had saved and invested when the economy hit bottom. They are learning to reassemble the pieces.

Our life was never the same after we left the Colorado church— and the pastorate. We encountered a lot of pain during our time there. The congregation divided over change; a staff member went to jail for embezzling funds, a youth pastor was terminated for improper behavior and eventually our church was hit by lightning and burned down. In our late-30s, we left Colorado feeling as though we had gone under for the last time. We were devastated; all washed up. Not so with God as our Navigator. With time, counsel, perseverance and prayer, we put the pieces back together and formed a new life.

These times of transitions are hard and uncertain. William

Bridges, in his book *Managing Transitions*, described the lost, abandoned, disoriented feeling "like Linus when his blanket is in the dryer."[6] Reassembling the pieces of a former life into a new one is part of understanding our Third Calling. It's a new opportunity.

FINALLY AND MOST IMPORTANT: TRUST

Trust God. Trust the one who knows what lies beyond the white water. Trust the One who will provide a better boat than the flimsy one you're using now. Trust the God of the Universe to make sense of the white waters.

Trust God and hang on. It's a great ride.

Our friend, Tina, is in the throes of white water. She recently posted this on her blog:

"Some of us must bear up under our horrible decisions. We've made mistakes and can't undo them. We've hurt people and can't unhurt them. Others of us have hurt ourselves, or we've been deeply wounded by loved ones or by broken systems and institutions and can't find the way to relief. So we go on our way and tell ourselves it doesn't matter, that it will be okay. But deep down, in the dark places of our hearts, it does matter and sometimes it's hard to sleep at night. We worry and deal with anxiety. Our hearts race. Our stomachs turn over. Our bodies get sick and can't seem to heal and we wonder if this is really what it's all about. Is this as good as it gets?

Yes. It is. This is life. It's filled with wonder and awe, beauty and mystery, love and hope and also with crushing disappointments and death, but always with new life."[7]

Navigating the white waters is part of life. Surviving them opens the possibilities to a new adventure, new life and a ton of stories to tell.

Consider: When have you experienced God's faithfulness through trial or loss?

CHAPTER 15

DEVELOPING YOUR PLAN
by Richard

"Planning is bringing the future into the present
so that you can do something about it now."
—Alan Lakein, Author,
Time-Management Coach

"Trust in the Lord with all your heart
and lean not on your own understanding;
in all your ways submit to him,
and he will make your paths straight."
—Proverbs 3:5-6

WE HAVE WRITTEN THIS BOOK to help you to consider the possibilities and opportunities in your Third Calling. By this point we hope you are convinced that you are uniquely designed for a purpose: a Third Calling Purpose.

As Will Rogers reminds us, however, "Even if you are on the right track, you'll get run over if you just sit there."[1]

It's time to turn our attention to developing a plan. A plan simply defines the steps necessary to accomplish your vision. It's moving from the cloud of imagination, or the abstract, to the concrete, specific goals and strategies to achieve them. It means taking action. Vision, without a plan, is simply a dream.

Goals, plans and vision will give you structure and motivation in your daily life. Of course, we must always be open to the unexpected;

the twists and turns enrich life and make it interesting.

CLARIFY YOUR PURPOSE

In chapter 3, we discussed the power of purpose in our Third Calling. As you increasingly understand how you are uniquely wired (design) and what it is that concerns you deeply (passion), your specific purpose in life will come into focus. Review what you learned through the recommended assessments or self-evaluation in this book.

Can you identify your Third Calling purpose? (Who are you and why are you here?) Begin by summarizing each component discussed in this book. Are there themes that run through your life review? Times where you identified satisfaction and fulfillment?

- What are your top five core values?
- What is your personality type?
- What are your top strengths or natural talents?
- What motivates you?
- What are your spiritual gifts?
- What do you truly care about—your passions?
- Where do you want to leave an impact?

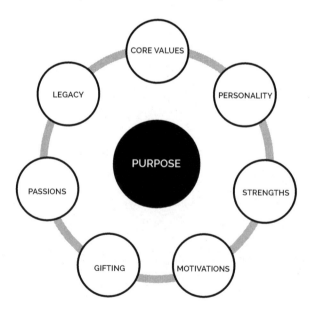

Complete the following paragraph to help put your purpose into words:

Knowing I care deeply about: my stories, passions, etc.

_____.

And, guided by: my core values _____

_____.

I will apply my God-given gifts and talents of: my personality,

strengths, spiritual gifts _____

_____.

And dedicate the next years of my life to: my purpose _____

_____.

With your Third Calling Purpose in mind, it is time to consider how to make it happen.

YOUR THIRD CALLING PLAN

If you want your plans to succeed, take the time to ask the hard questions and commit the answers to writing.

1. What is it you want to do? What is your goal?
   - Whom are you going to serve?
   - What problem are you going to address?
   - What need are you going to meet?
2. How are you going to do it?
   - What actions are required to complete it?
   - Put the actions in outline form in writing.
3. What resources do you need to accomplish your goals?

- Do you need money? Technical assistance? Materials?
- How will you secure these resources? Where? Who?

4. Who is going to help you accomplish your goal/idea?
   - Is there someone to hold you accountable to your plan?
   - Do you need professional assistance? Employees? Consultants?
   (Refer to Chapter 16—"Enlisting Your Team" for more suggestions.)

5. How will you track your progress?
   - Put due dates on your calendar, Evernote, or other helpful software
   - Write periodic summaries and updates (send them to those holding you accountable or to yourself)
   - Celebrate the completion of each step or accomplishment

SAMPLE PLAN

Here's an illustration of a specific Third Calling plan:

1. What do I want to do?
   a. I want to fight human trafficking in the Seattle metro area.
   b. I want to serve the young girls living in the Aurora bridge district.
   c. I want to understand the issues of trafficking and prevention.

2. How am I going to do it?
   a. I will apply to volunteer at the One Cup Coffee House where many of these girls come for help.

    b. I will complete the training offered at the Coffee House ministry by January 4. (Time frame)

3. What resources do I need:
    a. Time—I will give one day a week.
    b. Education and training—formal training through ministry; informal training through personal reading and study.
    c. Initially, I will donate to the Coffee House ministry out of my own funds, but eventually, I would like to be involved in fundraising.

4. Who is going to help me?
    a. The Volunteer Director at the One Cup Coffee House Ministry.
    b. My wife will hold me accountable for scheduling my time.

5. How will I track progress?.
    a. By putting the training dates on my calendar.
    b. Scheduling time to study volunteer training materials.
    c. Completing training and tests required to volunteer.
    d. Scheduling one day per week to volunteer. At the end of each volunteer day, write a short summary of people met, encounters with young girls.
    e. Celebrating accomplishments, including passing tests.

THIRD CALLING DIMENSIONS

Typically, when people speak of a plan for retirement, they think of a financial plan. The Third Calling is about more than money; it's about empowering your dreams and passions. It's not just making a better version of you; it's about making the world a better place. It's about bringing God glory.

Many dimensions of our lives would benefit from developing a Third Calling plan. Consider what goals and dreams you might develop for your health and fitness, family and relationships, spiritual growth, community involvement, or lifelong learning and education. Start small. Identify one goal for every area of your life that will help you fulfill your overall Third Calling purpose.

What's stopping you? Just do it.

> *"A good battle plan that you act on today*
> *is better than a perfect one tomorrow."*
> —General George S. Patton

> *"May He grant you your hearts desires and fulfill all your*
> *plans."*
> —Psalm 20:4 TLB

Consider: Draw a timeline with a starting point called "now" and an ending point called "goal." Mark three things that need to be done between those points.

CHAPTER 16

ENLISTING YOUR TEAM
by Richard

"... Won't you please, please help me? Help me!"
—John Lennon and Paul McCartney

"So encourage each other and build each other up,
just as you are already doing."
—1 Thessalonians 5:11 NLT

THERE ARE NUMEROUS THOUGHTS AS to why John Lennon wrote such desperate lyrics as those in the song *Help!* [1] One thing is certain—both the song and the movie made a ton of money for the Fab Four.

Help! is a great fight song for those of us following our Third Calling. We simply cannot go forward alone. We need the support and expertise of others to excel.

Leona and I are encouraged by enlisting a team to surround us with support, advice, insights and accountability. "No man is wise enough by himself." [2] (Plautus) This is particularly the case in our Third Calling adventures. Whether we are leading a movement, starting a new business, or serving in a new venture, we need a team to get us there.

We take the flame image of our Re-Ignite logo—lighting the flame of passion and purpose in our life—and apply it to the idea of enlisting a team. We call it our Campfire Circle. Nothing brings out honesty and accountability like a group of friends gathered around a campfire. Vulnerability and a willingness to learn emerge from the darkness of the night and the brilliance of the fire.

There are four kinds of people we need at our campfire.

1. Prayer partners.

People who will pray for us are essential. No matter where we are in our faith walk and spiritual journey, we need others who can articulate our needs. We are fortunate to have several such people, especially Gene and Linnea. This exceptional couple are both in their 80s and are incredibly fun to be with. They are also people who understand the power of prayer. They have been special in our lives ever since we connected over our shared love for Sweden. They embraced our vision to encourage Swedish Boomers and they committed to praying for us daily. They spread out the map of Sweden and walked the land with us in their thoughts and prayers. They welcomed us to their small group, a gathering of twelve people also committed to prayer and ministry. Over the years, this group has prayed us to and through many countries, ministry opportunities and personal challenges. There is absolutely no way you can succeed in a Third Calling without people praying for you. Share your vision, be specific about your needs and make a special place for those who come to your circle on their knees.

2. Listeners.

Your Third Calling journey is enriched when you share it with people who take the time to actually listen to your ideas, thoughts and schemes. Leona tends to have way too many ideas. Some of them are outrageous, especially the ones she has in the middle of the night. It always helps to have a sounding board to bounce ideas off and see if they have merit, are possible or should be filed away for another day.

Finding good listeners is like searching for treasure. When you find a good listener, seat them near you at your campfire. They'll watch the flame ignite as you talk and share. And then, when the time is right, they'll give you insight, truth, a dose of reality—and hope.

"This is the problem with dealing with someone who is actually a good listener. They don't jump in on your sentences, saving you from actually finishing them, or talk over you, allowing what you do manage to get out to be lost or altered in transit. Instead, they wait, so you have to keep going."
—Sarah Dessen, *Just Listen* [3]

3. Mentors.

Invite mentors to your campfire circle—lots of them. Mentors are more experienced or more knowledgeable people who can instruct, inform and guide you in your Third Calling.

Some mentors can be physically present, such as professors, pastors or entrepreneurs. Others are writers and their words, filled with experience and wisdom, teach and guide.

Being intentional about having mentors on your team is important. We've identified some incredible mentors, mostly skilled authors and cutting edge thinkers. We want to be constantly challenged to consider every angle of our Third Calling.

"One of the greatest advantages of mentors is the ability to see ahead what others cannot see and to help them navigate a course to their destination."
—John Maxwell

4. Professionals.

If your Third Calling is to start a new business, write a book, create a new product, or launch a service organization, you will need professional assistance to succeed and excel. Be focused on what help you need and invite them to your Campfire.

When we launched Re-Ignite, we knew we needed help getting our message out to the world. We hired a web designer to develop a first-rate website. We hired a film producer to create a movie (*Musical Chairs*); secured editors and publishers for our first book (*Amazing Grays*), as well as this one. We took classes from professionals about aging, computer software, fund raising and writing.

Professional or technical assistants have the more expensive seats at your Campfire Circle, but they are critical to the success of your Third Calling.

Enlist a team that believes in you and all that you bring to your Third Calling. The fire will blaze as your team stokes it with life, passion, advice and prayer.

"Alone we can do so little; together we can do so much."
—Helen Keller

Consider: Whom might you invite
to your Campfire Circle?

CHAPTER 17
FINDING YOUR VOICE
by Leona

*"Strive to find your own voice, because the longer you wait to begin,
the less likely you are to find it at all."*
—Professor John Keating
Dead Poets Society[1]

*"Speak up for those who cannot speak for themselves;
ensure justice for those being crushed.
Yes, speak up for the poor and helpless,
and see that they get justice."*
—Proverbs 31:8-9 NLT

AS A CHILD I TENDED to mumble, making it hard for others to hear and understand me. I often talked to the floor rather than project my message up and out to the world. I remember my mother prodding me to face my audience and use, what she called, my "BIG voice."

I think of that advice now, when in my Third Calling, I am so anxious for others to hear our message.

Everyone wants to be heard in some way or another. We realized this recently when we were subjected to the questionable artistry of Karaoke. While trying to relax in the hot tub, a DJ at the poolside restaurant announced it was time for any willing singer in the audience to take the microphone. I still cringe remembering men and women trying to emulate Celine Dion or Brad Paisley.

Most of their voices screeched and squawked like banshees.

Somewhat more on key than Karaoke participants, are the competitors on popular talent shows such as *American Idol* or *The Voice*. The gifted move on to compete in Hollywood, hoping for a chance to record a hit and become a star. Most contestants return home to sing in bars, choirs or in their showers. Each one tries to find his voice; tries to be heard above the rest.

Finding your voice in the Third Calling is more significant than belting out an oldie, winning a talent contest or speaking loud enough for others to hear. It's about knowing what you stand for, what you believe in and the difference you want to make in the world. And then doing what one needs to do to be heard.

Voice comes from the Latin word "vocare"—meaning to call or invoke. When we truly find our voice, we are asking people to not only hear us but to follow our passion.

Announcing she would run for the office of U.S. President, Hillary Clinton told a New Hampshire audience, "I've listened to you and, in the process, I found my own voice." In her Third Calling, she heard the needs of others, projected her "big voice," and took action.

HEARING YOUR OWN VOICE

Todd Henry, founder of the Accidental Creative and author of *Louder Than Words: Harness the Power of Your Authentic Voice*, suggests to develop your authentic voice, you must cultivate three things in your life:

1. A strong sense of identity.

Who are you? What gives you meaning? This concept is foundational in the Re-Ignite process. Discovering your unique design—your personality, strengths, gifts and passions—is critical to finding your voice.

2. A consonant vision.

Where are you going? What is your desired outcome? What

impact do you want to make?

3. Mastery.

How will you get there? What do you need to know and be able to do to fulfill your calling?

Henry states, "A strong, authentic, compelling voice is the expression of identity, guided by vision and achieved through mastery."[2]

He adds that we must uncover our voice, develop it and then bravely use it. What timely advice for those responding to and living their Third Calling. Now is no time to be silent or passive regarding the issues, people or causes that God has placed deep in our hearts.

FINDING OUR VOICE

This book is a tangible expression of Richard and I finding our voice. We heard our generation calling for a new model of aging—both in the culture and in the church. We explored our unique identity and realized that together we have abilities and strengths to understand challenges, identify possibilities and chart a course for action.

We first found our voice through writing. Words are powerful ambassadors of a message and we utilize them in every way we can. Through writing, we exposed the "backstage" of church life (*Leadership Journal*); challenged the stereotypes of aging in magazine articles, blogs, newsletters and books; unveiled new ideas on our website, and in white papers, proposals and business plans; and provided a structure for life planning through our Re-Ignite curriculum. Writing allows us to articulate our feelings and thoughts, share our insights and knowledge and state our opinions and beliefs. The written word has been an expression of our voice.

Additionally, we have found our voice through speaking. We seldom turn down an opportunity to share our message, whether with one person or to a packed house. Words spoken can change the course of history—and they can change lives. We have a message and it pops out nearly every time we open our mouths. We also produced a short film about finding your Third Calling entitled *Musical Chairs*. The movie speaks our message for us in a creative way.

Finally, we have found our voice through mobilizing a movement. We are doing this by utilizing social media, networking and facilitating Re-Ignite events. We know that our generation has been given so much, including vast holdings of money, education, experience and time. When we find our collective voices, we can answer deep spiritual questions, meet innumerable social needs and change the world. We are unashamedly asking our Boomer peers to join us in bravely using our gifts and talents to impact lives. We invite you to join the Re-Ignite Movement.

OTHERS WHO HAVE FOUND THEIR VOICE

Moses is famous for his reluctance to find and use his voice. God used a one-of-a-kind, irresistible approach to call Moses out of the desert and back into leadership—a burning bush (Exodus 3). God promises to give him a powerful voice, to which Moses responds, "Oh, my Lord. I am not eloquent, either in the past or since you have spoken to your servant, but I am slow of speech and tongue." To which the Lord responds, "Who has made man's mouth? Go and I will be with your mouth and teach you what you shall speak." Moses protests, "Oh, my Lord, please send someone else." (Exodus 3:10-13 ESV)

After some tense and angry moments, God agrees to send Moses' brother, Aaron, along with him to be his mouthpiece. Together they travel to argue their case before Pharoah. Aaron spoke the Lord's words—Moses hadn't quite found his voice yet.

Eventually, the Israelites are released from bondage and they begin their long and circuitous journey to the Promised Land.

Ultimately, Moses finds his voice. The opening words of the book of Deuteronomy say it all: "These are the words that Moses spoke to all Israel beyond the Jordan wilderness." The speeches go on for years and thirty-three chapters. God gave Moses a message and Moses found his voice.

> *"And there has not arisen a prophet*
> *since in Israel like Moses."*
> —Deuteronomy 34:10

Beaten down by a past of trauma, pain and shame, Trisha was nearly always quiet and withdrawn. Interactions were painful and public speaking was out of the question. Then she experienced "story ropes," a life review technique developed by Marge Malwitz and used by Marcia Carole and The Creative Call.[3] Using fabric strips of many colors and designs tied on a cord, participants tell their life story. Trisha not only found her own release from emotional bondage, but she also began teaching others the same method. She has traveled the world, teaching abused and neglected women the simple art of telling their story through textiles.

Trisha found her voice.

Rosa Parks was the granddaughter of former slaves. Throughout her young life, she experienced racial discrimination, first hand. She attended segregated, under-resourced schools. She eventually dropped out to care for family members. On December 1, 1955, after working a long day as a seamstress in a Montgomery department store, she boarded a metro bus to travel home. Somewhere along the route, the bus driver noted there were white passengers standing in the aisle. He stopped the bus and asked four seated passengers to give up their seats. All four were black. Three complied, but not Rosa. She found her voice. When the driver demanded she give her seat to a white passenger, she replied, "I don't think I should have to stand up." Later she remarked that she didn't refuse because she was physically tired, she was just tired of giving in.

The rest is history.

Rosa Parks found her voice.

YOUR VOICE

What message has God given you to share with the world? To stand up for? To speak for those who cannot speak for themselves?

Find your big voice and use it. It's required for your Third Calling.

> *"Our lives begin to end the day we become*
> *silent about things that matter."*
> —Martin Luther King Jr.

> *"In life, finding a voice is speaking and living the truth.*
> *Each of you is an original. Each of you has a distinctive voice.*
> *When you find it, your story will be told. You will be heard."*
> —John Grisham, Author

Consider: If you were given a microphone and asked to say one thing you want the world to know, what would you say?

CHAPTER 18

SWIMMING AGAINST THE STREAM
by Richard

"The man who is swimming against the stream knows the strength of it."
—President Woodrow Wilson

*"Don't become so well-adjusted to your culture
that you fit into it without even thinking."*
—Romans 12:2, The Message

SUNSHINE! THE VERY THOUGHT OF radiant sunbeams will awaken a Pacific Northwesterner from his hibernation.

It was November, and while our friends at home were opening umbrellas and commuting from work in the dark, we were luxuriating in the warmth of the Arizona sun. Our cells guzzled in the vitamin D while our dry souls re-hydrated in rays of renewal.

The morning marked the beginning of a new adventure for Leona and me. Two days earlier I said farewell to our church where I had served on staff for 10 years. Deciding it was time to follow our hearts and calling, we left a job, sold our house, and now we were ready to re-engage in developing Re-Ignite, a ministry division of our non-profit organization ChurchHealth we founded 20 years earlier. While walking in the sun-drenched morning, our conversations were animated, filled with dynamic ideas and vibrant optimism. We were ready to embark upon our Third Calling!

Then, without warning, our daydreams were interrupted by one word.

An oncoming jogger smiled and in a friendly manner asked, "Enjoying your retirement?"

"I'm NOT retired!" I responded with frustration as she sprinted by without waiting for an answer.

"I'm NOT retired!" I repeated, as she left my sight.

"Doggone it. I am not retired."

I suppose the assumption made should be expected. We were plunked in the middle of a beautiful retirement community in Arizona for a month. I was about to turn 65 and would clearly qualify to be a resident.

Nevertheless, I am not retired. I work full-time as President of my organization. I'm ready for fresh challenges, creative experiences and dazzling innovation. I have re-ignited a passion to serve my generation. I am refocusing my energies to help others discover their purpose in life. I'm following my Third Calling and traveling the world with a message.

Come to think of it, I, like most of my Boomer peers, don't like the word, "retired." While it typically describes someone who has left his job or career at a prescribed age (like 65), it also conjures up images of withdrawal, receding or being asked to sit on the bench like a struck-out baseball batter.

Embarking on my Third Calling, I felt as though I was swimming against the stream; and I am not alone. Marc Freedman, CEO of Encore, understands: "Millions of people are hitting a turning point in life, asking the big questions, thinking about what's next. They face a society that seems determined to shunt them into familiar categories even if they are ill-fitting traps."[1]

A year following that encounter with the jogger, Leona and I had the opportunity to spend another month near Sun City, Arizona, where we focused on writing this book. Every morning we took a walk in the sun before hitting our computers for the day. All along our route we observed people playing golf, tennis, shuffleboard, riding bikes, walking and lining up for pickle ball tournaments. Later in the day we visited the pool where people were sunbathing, swimming and playing water volleyball. In the evening we found others playing cards, Bunko, billiards, assembling jigsaw puzzles in the activity center and enjoying Happy Hour and Early Bird dinners. The posters around the community center advertised a variety of entertainment. One night, an Elvis concert, another the music of the 70s, and yet another a Chocolate Ball, complete with dancing and decadent desserts. There were multiple bus trips and tours available to enjoy. One never runs out of fun things to do in the Valley of the Sun.

The development of retirement communities in and around Sun City is a fascinating study. What happened in the 1960s changed the landscape of Arizona and it completely altered the paradigm of retirement.

According to Freedman:

"The Del Webb Corporation, in the late 50s and early 60s was marketing the retirement vision around the life of leisure in opening Sun City, Arizona. Prior to old age pension plans and social security, people worked until they were disabled or they died. But with more secure retirement plans in place, the focus shifted and Del Webb was at the forefront of that movement toward a more leisure-oriented retirement." [2]

On opening day, developers wondered if anyone would show up. They planned for 10,000 guests; more than 100,000 people came to see this new model of retirement. The rest is history. The ideal of a successful retirement was now clear: Sell your home in the cold and snowy north (or better yet keep it and be a snow bird) and move to the Sun Belt where you can enjoy a life of leisure. Marc Freedman explains:

"Beginning in the 1950s we turned that stage of life from a dreaded desert to a cherished destination, transforming it into a cornerstone of the American Dream. A leisured retirement became a symbol of a life well lived and whoever got there first deemed all the more successful. In reality, that seemingly magical transformation was actually the result of a combination of interests that brilliantly fashioned this stage—marketeers who sold the "golden years" ideal. We built it and they came, for decades on end." [3]

My life story intersects with the transformation of the Valley of the Sun. In 1965, my family packed up our entire household and moved from Kalispell, Montana to Phoenix, Arizona. I was a freshman in high school. We made the journey down Highway 93 with six of us crammed into the car. Our belongings would follow later. At that time there were 750,000 people in the valley, today it is home to 4.3 million people. In 1960, five years before we arrived, the Del Webb Corporation opened the first Sun City development. The original sign still stands at the entrance welcoming you to "Sun City: the original Fun City."

In 1987, twenty-two years after our move to Phoenix, my parents bought a condo in Sun Village, a gated retirement community west of Sun City. At that time, there was nothing west of them but desert and speculators. Today developments are springing up all throughout the Valley seeking to lure a fresh new crop of retirees.

During our recent stay in my parents' Sun Village condo, we were trying to stay focused and write. We watched streams of retirees in their golf carts zip past us. I have to admit occasionally I was tempted to trade my keyboard in exchange for a putter. Instead, I am swimming against the stream.

I am focused on what's next: my Third Calling.

SUBVERTING THE DOMINANT PARADIGM

In bright, colorful letters, the bumper sticker on the car in front of me caught my attention:

SUBVERT THE DOMINANT PARADIGM

It's the perfect rallying cry for those of us who are discovering and living our Third Calling. We have to subvert (undermine its power; overthrow) the dominant (most influential) paradigm (model or pattern) called "retirement." While, clearly, we are enjoying this season of life and the freedom it affords, we are not content to withdraw or disengage from our communities, families, or the world. What will it take?

1. Understanding the big picture.

How has such a model of leisure become the definition of retirement and this season of life? Certainly, all of us want to enjoy the rewards of our labor and we do need to rest, reflect, relax and recuperate from years spent working. But, as a result of the old marketing schemes for places like Sun City, an entire generation was sold on the idea that this stage of life is a time for withdrawal and leisure. Boomers are not too sure about that script. Most want to age with purpose and possibility. According to J. Walker Smith and Ann Clurman, authors of *Generation Ageless*,[4] Boomers universally share three foundational beliefs about this season of life:

- Youthfulness: A belief in an ageless engagement with life that is active, spirited and exuberant.
- Impact: A desire to have an enduring influence in making a difference.
- Possibility: A sense of personal development built upon empowerment and continuous progression.

Can these beliefs, ideals and values of the Boomer generation subvert the dominant paradigm that is so deeply engrained in our culture?

2. Seeking a new vision.

Marc Freedman says we need a "fresh map." He calls for the creation of a new stage between the end of the middle years and the beginning of retirement and old age—an encore stage of life. Dr. William Thomas, geriatrician and author of *Second Wind* [5] is on a nationwide tour called "The Age of Disruption." He asks a profound question, "What if nearly everything we think we know about aging is wrong?" If we are to subvert the dominant paradigm, we need a new vision and enlightened perspective.

3. Speaking of this new stage of life in new and optimistic ways.

Ken Dychtwald, noted gerontologist and author, illustrates this in his book, *With Purpose: Going from Success to Significance in Life and Work*: "This period of life may be the ideal time for fresh starts and late blooming with new dreams and goals, of intellectual growth, new relationships, vitality and contribution." [6]

4. Committing to lead a resistance.

Today's Boomers have the potential to fulfill many of the unrealized hopes and dreams of their earlier days. The 1960's generation, known for countering the culture of its time, has a second chance to subvert the dominant paradigm. Instead of bucking the political, economic and technological systems in western cultures, Boomers now can challenge the predominant attitudes that discriminate against and limit the possibilities of aging. We can model new ways to live a long time with purpose and passion. We can experience our Third Calling with confidence and commitment.

Christian Boomers have an even greater responsibility than anyone in our generation to lead a resistance. Following the Bible's instructions, we believe we should, first of all, value the sacredness of all of life, from beginning to end (Psalm 139). Second, we understand our time is short and we must work now (John 9:4). Third, we understand we should take care of those in need, including the poor, the widows, orphans, prisoners, those who are ill, and those who are lost (Jeremiah 22:3). Last, we are commanded to share the good news (gospel) with everyone in the world. (Matthew 28:16-20, John 3:16).

Having a Christian worldview inherently means swimming against the stream. Believing that aging has purpose, worth and value requires us to subvert the dominant paradigm of our culture, and sometimes our church. It may come at personal cost. Living your Third Calling is about doing what God wants you to do—what he has created you to do—for the rest of your life.

Swimming against the stream and subverting the dominant paradigm means rejecting culture's expectation that we withdraw or retire in our mid to late 60s. How do you view your years ahead? Leona and I, through our ministry of Re-Ignite, have developed a curriculum and a process to provide people with a map to discover their individual Third Calling. This book illustrates the Re-Ignite process and give you fresh insights and direction for how you can subvert the dominant paradigm and discover your Third Calling.

MUSICAL CHAIRS

A few years ago, we decided to produce a short film to communicate our subversive message. Our son, Jonathan, is an independent filmmaker; he agreed to help us. We shared our vision for challenging the dominant paradigm of retirement. Jonathan and his friend, Bryan, wrote a script, hired a cast, directed and filmed the 9-minute movie entitled *Musical Chairs*.[7] The film features Bill on the day of his retirement. He attends the traditional retirement party, is greeted by colleagues over cake and champagne and then exits the office and his career into a hallway, with the door slamming shut behind him. He looks down the hallway and sees a door marked "RETIREMENT." Cautiously he opens the door and enters the room, only to see a group of retirees playing the game, *Musical Chairs*. When the music stops, each one hurries to a seat. Bill finds his seat in front of a poster displaying a golfing scene. The loser of the round shuffles off stage and goes into mystical fog. The music starts again and Tom, a newly retired friend, enters the room. Bill, escaping the room, warns Tom as he leaves, "Don't do it, Tom! It's a trap!" He flees from the Retirement Room and sits down in the empty hallway. He stares at his gold retirement watch and you can feel his confusion and despair. A mysterious gentleman appears in the corridor carrying a box of tools and some wood. He instructs him to follow the directions and build something. With the help of others, Bill constructs a new door. When opened, it leads to a new hallway with more doors, each one labeled with opportunities for the future. They include education, missions, mentoring, service and even marriage. Bill discovers there is more to this season of life than playing *Musical Chairs* in the Retirement Room.

Our vision for the film was to challenge the prevailing model of retirement. *Third Calling* is our attempt to swim against the stream and subvert the dominant paradigm. We are living it, but occasionally, we wonder if we will eventually "be shunted into familiar categories even if they are ill-fitting traps." (Freedman)

THE BIG QUESTIONS

Is this season granted to our generation solely for our own pleasure and leisure, as the marketers would have us believe?

Is God calling us to experience more?

Is there an opportunity for you to have a Third Calling that goes beyond the pursuit of leisure as an end in itself?

Are you ready to swim against the stream? Are you willing to subvert the dominant paradigm?

What will that look like for you?

What are you doing the rest of your life?

Consider: Where in your life do you encounter negative or limiting messages about aging and growing older?

CHAPTER 19
LIVING A LEGACY
by Leona

"My life is my message."
—Mahatma Gandhi

"Those who say they live in God should live their lives as Jesus did."
—I John 2:6 NLT

HAVE YOU EVER VISITED THE "happiest place on earth?" Did you find it to be a place where dreams really can come true?

For over six decades, millions of people have experienced the legacy of one man, Walt Disney. We are heirs to his passion for fantasy, curiosity, imagination and even whimsy. We can explore islands, speed through the black skies of space, scream with fear and excitement in haunted mansions and giggle with princesses in fairy tale castles. We experience Walt Disney's legacy in magical places bearing his name: Disneyland and Disneyworld. Walt Disney left us a part of himself that will go on for as long as children have imaginations.

The Dachau Concentration Camp outside Munich, Germany stands in sharp contrast. We recently visited this dreadful place, Adolph Hitler's legacy. At Dachau, we experienced the horrors of power, control, wickedness and evil that went terribly and incomprehensibly wrong. Hitler left a legacy that will be remembered as long as humankind recognizes injustice, hate and evil.

Both men built places that continue speaking their legacy long after their deaths. While alive, they lived their legacies: Hitler demonstrated cruel hate throughout his tyrannical reign; Disney warmly welcomed us weekly into his "Wonderful World of Disney."[1] They both lived and left a legacy.

Some legacies are instantly recognized through a product bearing a name: Ford, Heinz, Coors, Hilton, Mary Kay and my personal favorite, Hershey. The mention of a name can tantalize our taste buds or make us yearn for a convertible ride. The legacy of the inventor or founder lives on in our senses.

Some legacies are acknowledged and celebrated by others. One of our most significant mentors was Dr. Vernon Grounds. As president of Denver Seminary when Richard was a student, Dr. Grounds invested time, energy and immeasurable wisdom into our lives. Hundreds of other men and women who passed through Dr. Grounds' life would say the same thing. His legacy lives on through the Counseling Center that bears his name. Another person having profound significance in our lives was Dr. John L. Mitchell, who served as pastor at Bethany Bible Church in Phoenix, Arizona. Today, in the center of the Dallas Theological Seminary's campus stands the Mitchell Ministry Center, dedicated to the memory of this churchman and theologian. Obviously, throughout the ages, countless buildings, memorials and statues have been erected to honor the significance of remarkable men and women. Leaving a legacy implies one has lived one.

As we consider our Third Calling, the concept of legacy becomes real. What images will our name raise in the minds of those who knew us? What will our children remember? Our grandchildren? What will they inherit from us?

LEAVING OR LIVING?

A bumper sticker frequently seen on RVs roaring down

interstates heading toward warmer climates says, "We are spending our children's inheritance." I used to think it was humorous, but as I consider what it means to leave a legacy, I'm beginning to wonder if we've focused more on leaving material goods than endowing a value-based legacy. Are we considering riches rather than relationships?

Leaving a legacy may mean giving large sums of money toward a cause, building, foundation, or scholarship. Living a legacy means investing in people.

Peter Strople, business executive and author, says "Legacy is not leaving something for people, it's leaving something *in* people."[2]

Investing in lives is dynamic, vital, enduring. It doesn't get spent. It doesn't run out. Living a legacy implies while we have breath, we are making choices, taking action, doing things that make a difference and investing in other lives.

My Grandma Thomas did not leave me tons of money when she died. In fact, I think the sum of my inheritance is a beautiful china dish I admired throughout my life. She did leave a legacy, however, one that she lived in front of me every day. I spent my entire childhood on my grandparents' farm in Wheatridge, Colorado where we raised corn, beans, tomatoes, strawberries, raspberries and of course, zucchini. I loved the harvest because it seemed as though there were unending amounts of luscious crops. As a small child, it never occurred to me how much work was involved in producing these fruits and vegetables. I thought it came easily. But, over the years, as I grew up and expanded my understanding of life, I began to grasp the beauty of her legacy.

One thing Grandma taught was whatever you do, you should do well. It started with showing me how seeds had to be carefully selected and purchased, then the dark fertile soil had to be tilled and prepared for planting; and then the seeds had to be planted the right depth and spaced apart just right—and in *straight* rows. In the days and weeks that followed, there was irrigating, hoeing, covering the plants during hail storms and the inevitable and tedious weeding. All of that before we could enjoy one bite of juicy corn on the cob.

Grandma's legacy was about more than hard work. It was also about love. While Grandma planted the beans in straight rows, she also planted them with a broad path right through the middle of the field. The path connected my house to hers. She welcomed me anytime I wanted to come over, which was often (especially if I thought we could make chocolate chip cookies).

Grandma endured great hardships in her 92 years, yet through her life, she never stopped trusting her Lord. She always taught me that the God of all creation was in control, that nothing surprised Him and that he loved us during times of pain as well as joy. By the time Grandma died, she had cared for and buried all of her sisters and brothers, her husband and one son. She had endured life's normal and extraordinary trials. When I would go through dark valleys in my life she reminded me of God's undying faithfulness.

My grandmother was not a preacher or an evangelist. She was a little farm woman from rural Colorado. But she lived a legacy of perseverance, generosity, accessibility, love and faith. The seeds she planted continue to produce fruit in the lives of her heirs living today.

INVESTING OUR THIRD CALLING

What we do in this season of life reflects what truly matters to us. The next generation cannot afford for us to believe our primary contributions are found in what money and property we leave behind. It's about living our legacy *today*—in this season of our lives. What are ways we can intentionally live a legacy?

1. Develop strong relationships with our family.

Mend any bonds that have broken between you and your adult children. Seek to understand and appreciate the adults your children have become. Senator Paul Tsongas, after receiving a terminal diagnosis, stated in his book, *Heading Home,* "No one on his deathbed has ever said, 'I wish I'd spent more time at the office.'" [3] The quote cuts to the heart of the matter.

2. Devote time and energy to your grandchildren and great-grand-children.

For many, caregiving for grandkids has become their primary purpose in the Third Calling. For others, it is a role that provides unending joy and also an opportunity for influence.

Be creative in ways you spend time. If you live a long distance from your grandkids, learn to Skype and FaceTime and Twitter—and any other means available to communicate with them. We recently discovered Voxer, an app that works like a free walkie-talkie. We can leave voice recordings for our grandkids now living overseas. It's a great way to stay connected and live our legacy on a daily basis.

Rather than only giving the latest video game or Lego set, consider giving gifts that have meaning. One Christmas, our daughter requested we give experiences rather than gifts. I loved the idea, so we purchased family memberships to the zoo and the Children's Museum. I designed some great gift certificates to give to the kids on Christmas day. While the family later enjoyed the gift that kept on giving, in the glee of opening gifts, there was a bit of disappointment. Our 4-year old grandson expressed honestly, "So, why didn't you give us a Christmas present, Grandma?" Fortunately, I did have a package or two to offer. It was a good reminder that wrapped within every gift, whether a toy or a membership, is a Grandparents' legacy.

Will you be remembered for giving a part of yourself along

with every gift?

3. Find a cause that makes a difference.

My cousin, Karen, lives and breathes kindness. She counsels and guides missionary candidates toward service in foreign lands. But she has another cause she devotes time and energy to—the protection of animals, especially dogs that have been mistreated or abused. She contributes time and strength to the Golden Retriever of the Rockies, a non-profit organization in Arvada, Colorado. No doubt, she is living her legacy as she helps the helpless.

4. Find a hurt to heal.

Living a legacy may mean bringing peace and reconciliation to a family or even a country. Earlier I mentioned our visit to Dachau, the concentration camp outside Munich, Germany. During that same trip, we visited Berlin. This city has a history of war and division, including the Cold War of the 1960s and the erection of a wall to segregate the Communist East from West Berlin. As we toured Berlin and walked freely through both East and West, we noted large cylinder-shaped displays dotted throughout the city. Each exhibit displayed a picture and story of someone or some group of people who had been discriminated against, even annihilated, during Berlin's history. The displays were intentional efforts to acknowledge the terrible acts of Germany's past and then move on.

Our efforts to bring reconciliation within our families, our communities and the world can, like the Berlin displays, become our living legacy.

5. Serve others.

There is no better way to live a legacy than in service to others. Whether it is volunteering in a school, starting a new ministry to the homeless, or caring for an elder parent or friend—giving of ourselves in service is living a legacy.

UNPRECEDENTED OPPORTUNITIES

Like no other generation before us, we have the chance to create and live our legacy. We can invest in our families and our world in ways limited only by our imaginations and fortitude.

"With today's great gains in longevity and health, there is now the opportunity for so many of us to do work that is real at a juncture when previous generations were sent to the sidelines. Today, we can do more even than leave a legacy. We can actually live one." [4]
—Marc Freedman, CEO, Encore.org

"Being the richest man in the cemetery doesn't matter to me....Going to bed at night saying we've done something wonderful...That's what matters to me." [5]
—Steve Jobs, Founder, Apple

Consider: Write three things
you want to be known for.

EPILOGUE

IMAGINING THE FUTURE–FINAL THOUGHTS
By Leona

In light of all this, here's what I want you to do, I want you to
get out there and walk—better yet, run!—on the road God
called you to travel. I don't want any of you sitting around on
your hands. I don't want anyone strolling off, down some path
that goes nowhere. You were all called to travel on the same road
and in the same direction, so stay together, both outwardly and
inwardly.
You have one Master, one faith, one baptism, one God and Father of all,
who rules over all, works through all, and is present in all.
But that doesn't mean you should all look and speak and act the same.
Out of the generosity of Christ, each of us is given his own gift.
Don't take such a gift for granted.
—Ephesians 4:1-13, 30 The Message

MORE THAN YOU CAN IMAGINE

Emotions nearly overwhelmed us when Richard and I took radical steps toward fulfilling our Third Calling. We were excited, apprehensive, fearful, calm, confident, brave, and terrified all at once. In reading this book, you have learned first-hand how God has led and directed us through the years and now to this season of life. You've read about our personal discoveries, accomplishments and failures, and you've glimpsed into the lives of others who are also finding purpose and passion in this season of life. Hopefully, in reading *Third Calling*, you've laughed out loud and perhaps shed a tear or two.

Our lives are not much different from yours. Yes, the circumstances and people and events are different, but the principles are the same: God has designed you for a purpose and he has an assignment for this season that only you can fulfill. Accomplishing your Third Calling will impact the world and make it a better place; ultimately, it will bring glory to God, your Creator.

I attended a leadership wives' gathering a few months before we jumped into leading Re-Ignite full-time. It was a craft-making day. Each one was given a piece of canvas, paints and plastic-stick-on letters. We were asked to think of a phrase, Bible verse or quote to depict in our artwork. Individuals chose a variety of sayings, including "Live, Love, Laugh" and "Where's the Coffee?" and "Be still, and know that I am God." When given the assignment, my favorite Bible verse, Ephesians 3:20 came to my mind. I applied the stick-on letters and painted over the canvas as instructed. I used bright lime-green paint. When the whole process was complete, I had a beautiful little framed canvas revealing the words, "More than you can imagine."

The small square plaque hangs above our dining table and reminds us that God has called us to experience his power, provision and plan every day. What he is doing in our lives is "more than we can imagine." How he has provided for us is "more than we can imagine." What He is going to do in your life is "more than you can imagine."

Our prayer is that the words in this book will challenge and encourage you to discover your Third Calling. God has a plan for what you are going to do the rest of your life. As a generation, we can do more together than any one of us can on our own.

It is more than you can imagine.

Now to him who is able to do immeasurably more than all we ask
or imagine, according to his power that is at work within us,
to him be glory in the church and in Christ Jesus
throughout all generations, for ever and ever! Amen.
—Ephesians 3:20-21

Consider: What 5-10 words do you want on a plaque hanging above your dining table?

NOTES

Chapter 1

1. *"What Are You Doing The Rest of Your Life?,"* lyrics by Alan Bergman and Marilyn Bergman and original music written by Michel Legrand for the 1969 film, *Happy Ending.*

Chapter 2 – Following The Call

1. Francis Schaeffer, *The God Who Is There*, InterVarsity Press, 1998, p. 169.
2. Westmont College website: http://www.westmont.edu/_offices/olp. Permission to use this information from the website was granted by the Office of Student Life.
3. Matthew 28:19-20a, New International Version
4. Chris R. Armstrong, *Leadership Journal*, Winter, 2013, p. 46.
5. Os Guinness, *Rising to the Call*, E-book, Thomas Nelson, 2008, p. 29, pp. 35-36.
6. Ephesians 4:12a, ESV
7. Parker J. Palmer, *Let Your Life Speak: Listening to the Voice of Vocation*, Jossey-Bass, 2000, p. 4.

Chapter 3 – Knowing Your Purpose

1. *Oxford Dictionary*, Oxford University Press, 2016 www.Oxforddictionaries. com
2. Richard Bach, *The Bridge Across Forever: A True Love Story.* William Morrow Company, 1984.
3. Richard Leider, *The Power of Purpose.* Berrett-Koehler Publishers, Inc. 2010, pp. 3, 6, 9.
4. Ibid, p. 22.
5. Lewis Carroll, *Alice's Adventures in Wonderland*, 1865.
6. Harold Koenig, M.D. *Purpose and Power in Retirement*, Temple Foundation Press, 2002, p. 7.
7. Ken Dychtwald, Ph.D., *With Purpose: Going from Success to Significance in Work and Life*, Collins Living/Harper Collins. 2009, p. 4.
8. Darren Poke, Executive Coach, www.betterlifecoaching.com.

Chapter 4 - Stepping Into Your Story

1. *The Voyage of Life*, Thomas Cole, 1842; Four paintings in the collection exhibited at the National Gallery of Art, 6th and Constitution Streets, Washington D.C.
2. Center for Disease Control, Health, United States, 2014, p. 4. "In 2013, life expectancy at birth in the United States for the total population is 78.8 years—76.4 years for males and 81.2 years for females.
3. Dychtwald, *With Purpose*, p. 76.
4. J. Walker Smith, *Generation Ageless*, Collins. 2007, p. 36.

5. Marc Freedman, *Encore*, Public Affairs, New York, p. 12.
6. Marc Freedman, *The Big Shift*, Public Affairs, 2011, p. 101.
7. Robert Butler, MD, *Age, Death and Life Review*, published by Harbor Light Hospice Volunteers. www.hlhvolunteers.com.
8. Gordon MacDonald, *The Resilient Life*, Nelson Books, 2004, p. 37.
9. Beth Sanders, LifeBio, www.LifeBio.com.
10. Marcia Carole, Story Ropes, featured on www.CreativeCall.net.
11. Sybil Towner, OneLifeMaps, www.onelifemaps.com.
12. Frederick Beuchner, *Now and Then: A Memoir of Vocation*, Harper One, 1991.

Chapter 5 – Pursuing Your Passion

1. For more about Encore and the Purpose Prizes visit www.Encore.org.
2. Ileana's Smile, www.lovelightandmelody.org.
3. Laurie Beth Jones, *The Path*, Hyperion Books, 1996, p. 58.

Chapter 6 - Awakening Your Dreams

1. *Rapunzel*. Author unknown. German fairy tale assembled by the Brothers Grimm, originally published in 1812.
2. *Tangled*. Movie produced by Walt Disney Movies. Released November 2010.
3. Catch the Wind Sailing Ministries, Will and Rebecca Stout, Founders. http://www.catchthewindsailingministries.org.

Chapter 7 – Clarifying Your Values

1. Bert Jacobs: "Gaining a 'Life is Good' Perspective." Keynote address at Ariba Live Conference 2014. https://vimeo.com/95404668.
2. *Schindler's List*, produced and directed by Steven Spielberg, based on the novel, *Schindler's Ark* by Thomas Keneally. Released November 30, 1993 by Universal Pictures.
3. Life is Good Foundation—http://www.lifeisgood.com.

Chapter 8 - Discovering Your Design

1. Rick Warren, *The Purpose Driven Life*, Zondervan, 2002, pp. 244-45.
2. *The Nanny Diaries*, directed by Shari Springer Berman and Robert Pulcini, produced by Weinstein Company, released by MGM, August 2007.
3. PeopleKeys provides DISC assessments and training. www.peoplekeys.com.
4. Description of DISC traits found at http://peoplekeys.com/about-disc/what-is-disc.
5. Elisa Hawkinson, *Calming Your Chaos*, Aviva Publishing, 2015.
6. Gallup Strengths Finder offers online assessments at www.gallupstrengthscenter.com. There are several Strengths Finder™ books available. In Re-Ignite, we utilize *Living Your Strengths: Discover Your God-given Talents* by Albert Winseman, D.Min., Curt Liesveld and Donald O. Clifton, Gallup Press, 2004.
7. MCORE is an online assessment available at www.motivationalcore.com.

Created by Joshua Miller, Ph.D.
8. SIMA®, System for Identifying Motivated Abilites. www.simainternational.com.
9. A spiritual gifts inventory is available at www.spiritualgiftstest.com.

Chapter 9 – Cultivating Your Creativity

1. Gene Cohen, M.D., Ph.D., author of *The Creative Age*, from a lecture at University of Washington entitled, "Mirror, Mirror, on the Wall: What is Aging After All?" May 27, 2009.
2. Roger Von Oechs, *A Whack on the Side of the Head*, Warner Books, 1983.
3. Richard Bergstrom, "Stunned by an Inside Job" & "The Pastor as Lightning Rod," Leadership Journal, Fall, Winter 1987.
4. Richard Bergstrom, *Mastering Church Finances*, Multnomah Press, 1996.
5. Leona & Richard Bergstrom, *Amazing Grays: Unleashing the Power of Age in Your Congregation*, ChurchHealth, 2000.
6. *Musical Chairs*, Produced by ChurchHealth, directed by Jonathan Bergstrom, SmallFire Films, 2006.

Chapter 10 – Unleashing Your Inner Entrepreneur

1. Os Guinness, *Rising to the Call*, Thomas Nelson, 2003, p. 8.
2. Ibid, p. 10.
3. *How to Start a Non-Profit Organization*, NOLO Press, 1995.
4. Sandra Deja, www.501c3book.com.
5. Bergstrom, *Amazing Grays*, ChurchHealth, 2000.
6. *Stranger than Fiction*, Columbia Pictures, 2006.
7. *Calling All Girls*, published in the 1930's for 72 years, became *Young Miss* magazine (late 1960s) then *Your Magazine* (YM), 1980s; ceased publication 2004.
8. http://www.wowonline.org/documents/OlderAmericansGenderbriefFINAL.pdf.
9. Amy Grossman, "7 Traits of Women Entrepreneurs", http://nabbw.com/member-articles/business/7-traits-of-women-entrepreneurs/

Chapter 11 – Hearing the One Who Calls

1. Dr. William Thomas. Blog post "Aging Super Power Number One, www.edenalt.org.
2. The Westminster Shorter Catechism.
3. Gary Thomas, *Sacred Pathways*, Grand Rapids, Michigan, Zondervan, 1996.
4. *Turn Your Eyes Upon Jesus*, written by Helen Lemmel, 1922. Public Domain.

Chapter 12 – Exploring New Worlds

1. Rick Steves European Travel Center, Edmonds, Washington.
2. Fairway Recreation Center, https://sunaz.com/fairway-center.
3. Road Scholar, https://www.roadscholar.org.

4. Seattle University: Search for Meaning Book Festival, https://www.seattleu.edu. searchformeaning.
5. The National Council on Aging (NCOA), https://www.ncoa.org.
6. American Society on Aging (ASA), http://www.asaging.org.
7. PBS, http://www.pbs.org.
8. *UP*, the movie, Disney 2009, http://movies.disney.com/up.

Chapter 14 – Navigating White Waters

1. Frank Sinatra, *That's Life*, arranged and conducted by Ernie Freeman.
2. *Sacred Journey*, Ward Tanneberg, Amazon, White Glove, 2016.
3. Society for the Study of Addiction, https://www.addiction-ssa.org.
4. CelebrateRecovery.com, a Christ-centered recovery program of Saddleback Church.
5. Alcoholics Anonymous, aa.com, an international fellowship of men and women who have had a drinking problem.
6. William Bridges, *Managing Transitions: Making the Most of Change*, Addison-Wesley Publishing Company, 1991.
7. Tina Osterhouse, tinabustamante.com.

Chapter 15 – Developing Your Plan

1. http://www.brainyquote.com/quotes/quotes/w/willrogers104938.html.

Chapter 16 – Enlisting Your Team

1. *Help!*, John Lennon and Paul McCartney, written in 1965.
2. Plautus, http://www.brainyquote.com/quotes/quotes/p/plautus159670. html.
3. Sarah Dressen, *Just Listen*, Penguin Group, 2006.

Chapter 17 – Finding Your Voice

1. Professor John Keating, *Dead Poets Society*. Screenplay by Tom Schulman. Touchstone Pictures, 1989
2. Todd Henry, *Louder Than Words: Harness the Power of Your Authentic Voice*, pp. 12-13.
3. TheCreativeCall.net.

Chapter 18: Swimming Against the Stream

1. Marc Freedman, *The Big Shift: Navigating the New Stage Beyond Mid-Life*, Public Affairs/Perseus Books, 2011, p. 52.
2. Marc Freedman, *Primetime: How Baby Boomers Will Redefine Retirement and Transform America*, Public Affairs/Perseus Books, 1999.
3. Freedman, *The Big Shift*, pp. 68-69.
4. J. Walker Smith and Ann Clurman, *Generation Ageless*, Collins Publishing, 2007, p. 29.
5. William Thomas, MD., *Second Wind*, Simon and Schuster, 2014. Quote is

taken from his website: www.drbillthomas.com.

6. Dychtwald, *With Purpose*, p. 4.
7. *Musical Chairs*, Screenplay by Jonathan Bergstrom and Bryan Gough. Produced by ChurchHealth, 2006

Chapter 19 – Living A Legacy

1. *Wonderful World of Disney*, premiered on ABC October 27, 1954.
2. Peter Strople, www.friendsofpeter.net.
3. Senator Paul Tsongas, *Heading Home*, Knopf, 1984
4. Marc Freedman, The Harvard Business Review, December 11, 2012, https://hbr.org/2012/12/dont-leave-a-legacy-live-one/
5. Steve Jobs, Founder, Apple, http://www.goodreads.com/quotes/445606-being-the-richest-man-in-the-cemetery-doesn-t-matter-to.

We are grateful to the many people who have participated in Re-Ignite events. With permission, we have included many of their stories as well as others' in this book. (Some illustrative examples we use are composites of several people and do not represent specific individuals.)

ACKNOWLEDGEMENTS

Our heartfelt gratitude to:

- Our adult children: Jonathan, and his wife Emily; and Lynnea, and her husband, Daniel. Thank you for your encouragement and prayers. Thank you for believing in us—even when we take risks and do crazy things.

- Audrey Anderson and Ruth Bergstrom, our mothers. Thank you for modeling what it means to walk by faith.

- Paul Muncey and Susan Hedding, our editors, graphic designers and friends. Thank you for contributing your time, expertise and insights to make *Third Calling* a reality.

- ChurchHealth and Re-Ignite board, partners and donors. Because of your generosity and faithfulness, we are able to follow our Third Calling to write, speak, coach and influence lives around the globe.

- The many people who participated in Re-Ignite events through the years. Thank you for sharing your life journeys with us. Many of the stories shared in this book are those of Re-Ignite participants.

- Our dads, grandparents, and other family heroes who are now in Heaven—still cheering us on.

- Our fellow Boomers. We're a rebellious bunch and together we just might change what growing older means.

Serving Him for a Lifetime,
Richard and Leona Bergstrom

ABOUT THE AUTHORS

Richard Bergstrom, D.Min.

Born January 10, 1950 in Kalispell, Montana, Richard is the middle child in a family of four other Boomer siblings. He received a B.A. degree in psychology from Westmont College in Santa Barbara, California; an M.Div. degree from Denver Seminary, Denver, Colorado, and a D.Min. degree from Western Seminary in Portland, Oregon. Richard has served as a lead pastor, executive pastor, denominational executive, and a church consultant. He is Founder and President of ChurchHealth, a non-profit organization promoting personal coaching and church consulting.

Leona Bergstrom

Leona, born in Denver Colorado in 1951, is the older of two children. She has a B.A. degree in Sociology from Westmont College, Santa Barbara, California. Leona has enjoyed a career in developing and managing social and health care programs for older adults and their families. She currently directs the ministry of Re-Ignite, a division of ChurchHealth.

Richard and Leona have served in ministry together for all 44 years of their marriage. In addition to the pastoral ministry, they developed effective programs for midlife and older adults in local churches and in national and international ministries. Together they wrote *Amazing Grays: Unleashing the Power of Age in Your Congregation* (2000), produced the short-film, *Musical Chairs* (2006), and released the book, *Third Calling*, in 2016. Both write articles for periodicals and have been published in *Leadership Journal* and *Mature Living*. Currently, Richard and Leona lead the ministry of Re-Ignite, and have developed curriculum, retreats and events. They are passionate about encouraging their peers, the Boomers, to hear and follow God's calling in this season of life.

Richard and Leona have two adult children and six grandchildren. They live in Seattle, Washington.

RE-IGNITE RESOURCES

Do you want to discover your Third Calling? We can help.
Re-Ignite provides resources to assist you in discovering and living your Third Calling. Visit www.Re-Ignite.net

1. **Re-Ignite Coaching**

   Re-Ignite staff offers one-to-one personal coaching. Personal coaching is particularly helpful during times of transition or exploration.

2. **Re-Ignite Speaking**

   Re-Ignite staff is available to speak to your community or church groups. Presentations are based on the principles discussed in Third Calling and are interactive, lively and challenging.

3. **Re-Ignite Events**

   Re-Ignite offers a variety of events, including:

   Re-Ignite Retreats

   Held at a conference center, camp, church or hotel, Re-Ignite Retreats are designed for 25-45 participants. Retreats are typically held on a Friday night, all-day Saturday and Sunday morning and feature presentations, large and small group discussions, assessments, times of solitude and reflection, and fellowship with others.

   Re-Ignite Experience

   Held in a church or similar facility, typically on a Friday evening through Saturday afternoon. Participants return home or stay at nearby hotels for lodging.

   Re-Ignite Exclusives

   Held in a smaller venue such as a vacation home, retreat center or private residence, Exclusives are designed for 4-10 participants.

   Re-Ignite Expeditions

   International events.

CONTACT US

www.Re-Ignite.net

Email: info@chonline.org

360-676-4824

Made in the USA
Middletown, DE
24 January 2017